FAT QUARTER
GIFTS

FAT QUARTER
GIFTS

25 projects to make from short lengths of fabric

Jemima Schlee

First published 2017 by
Guild of Master Craftsman Publications Ltd
Castle Place, 166 High Street, Lewes,
East Sussex, BN7 1XU

A catalogue record for this book is available from the
British Library.

Publisher Jonathan Bailey
Production Manager Jim Bulley
Senior Project Editor Sara Harper
Editor Cath Senker
Managing Art Editor Gilda Pacitti
Art Editor Manisha Patel
Photographer Emma Sekhon
Step Photography Jemima Schlee
Picture Credit Cover illustrations: Shutterstock/Ohn Mar

Colour origination by GMC Reprographics
Printed and bound in Malaysia

A note on measurements
The imperial measurements in these projects are
converted from metric. While every attempt has
been made to ensure that they are as accurate
as possible, some rounding up or down has been
inevitable. For this reason, it is always best to
stick to one system or the other throughout a
project: do not mix metric and imperial units.

CONTENTS

INTRODUCTION

I have myriad pieces of fabrics of various sizes and endless colours stored in a chest of drawers: fat quarters I have simply not been able to resist buying and smaller pieces left over from finished projects. If, like me, you are addicted to fabric, you too are bound to have a selection of fabulous offcuts and cherished remnants just crying out to be used.

Here are 25 stylish projects to help you to make the most of these marvellous materials. The perfect way to use such a treasure trove is to make presents to give on birthdays, celebrations and anniversaries, or for no reason at all – just for the pleasure of giving. Giving a gift is almost as good as receiving one, and presenting someone with a hand-made item you've crafted especially for them is even more satisfying.

You can personalize the projects in this book by carefully choosing colours and patterns from the multitude of fat quarters on offer. Colour and pattern can completely alter the character of your gift, so choose fabrics with the recipient in mind. Any smaller fabric requirements can be found in your stash, which may range from recent dress-making projects and older treasures, to long-grown-out-of children's garments – all of them will add character and history to your gifts.

A fat quarter is simply half a yard of fabric cut in half again vertically, and in this book it refers to an 18 x 22in (46 x 56cm) maximum piece of fabric. Sizes do vary, depending upon the width from which the fabric is cut, so bear this in mind when working out your fabric requirements. All the makes in this book are ideal for cotton and linen fabrics; try to choose fabrics of very similar weights if you are combining more than one. Most of these projects are relatively small, so heavyweight fabrics are not very suitable – the seams and corners can become bulky and hard to work with.

I hope you enjoy making your fat quarter gifts as much as I have. I'm sure that the satisfaction of making use of a treasured piece of fabric will be matched by the pleasure you will give when you offer your lovingly made gift.

Jemima

THE BASICS

MATERIALS & EQUIPMENT

Each project in this book lists all the materials and equipment you will need. For all projects, you will need a sewing machine and thread, a sewing needle, pins, sharp dress-making scissors, a pen or fabric marker and an iron. Here are some tips for storing and using your materials and equipment.

YOUR WORKSPACE Make sure you work in a well-lit environment. If natural lighting is poor, use a lamp set to the other side of your working hand to avoid working in shadow. If you are lucky enough to have a dedicated workspace, keep an ironing board and iron at the ready.

If space is limited, press your work with the iron on a folded towel or piece of thick fabric in the corner of your work surface to save space.

MEASURING Use either a measuring tape or a ruler, but whichever you use, make sure you consistently use imperial or metric measurements and do not mix the two.

SCISSORS Ideally, you should have two pairs of sewing scissors. A small pair of sharp, pointed scissors is essential for cutting threads and trimming corners and curves. Then you

need a pair of sewing shears, or even two pairs in different sizes. These have long blades and a bent handle so that the scissors can rest on the table while cutting, keeping the fabric flat. The blades should be kept sharp. Make sure your scissors are used solely for fabrics so that no one uses them to cut paper.

SEAM RIPPER A seam ripper is used for unpicking stitches. Insert the pointed blade underneath the thread to be cut. Push it forward against the thread and the blade will cut it. It's possible to run the blade along a line of stitching between the two layers of fabric and cut all the stitches in one movement, but it takes a bit of skill to prevent tearing.

PINS AND PINNING Pinning and tacking seams ensure the fabric will not slip when stitching, so you can produce a neat, straight seam. Use pins with coloured glass heads, which are easy to spot in fabric. Place pins at right angles to the stitching line if you want to machine stitch over them and avoid having to tack or baste.

NEEDLES Sharps have a relatively large eye, making them fairly easy to thread for hand stitching. Embroidery needles are thicker and have a larger eye to accommodate the thicker embroidery thread.

THREADS You can use large jam jars to store your threads. Group them in colours to reduce tangles and speed up the search for a specific shade.

BOBBINS Keep little pillboxes of fully charged bobbins in a variety of colours – this way you can pop a fresh, full bobbin in when you've run out, rather than having to unthread and thread the machine to fill one. If sewing two different-coloured fabrics together, to make your stitching less visible, it can be useful to sew with one colour threaded on the machine needle, and another colour in the bobbin.

FABRICS Choose natural fibres whenever possible, such as linens, cottons or linen/cotton mixes. Mix and match oddments to make up the amounts required for the projects. Natural fibres are best washed before use to avoid problems with shrinkage later. For trims and ties use simple traditional rickrack, piping cord, herringbone and woven tapes, 100% cotton threads and plain buttons in coordinating colours.

TECHNIQUES

The majority of the projects in this book involve basic sewing techniques, both by hand and machine. Listed here is all the information you will need to complete the projects, including some basic instructions and some specific tips to help your sewing go smoothly.

PREPARING TO SEW

TEMPLATES AND PATTERNS

When your project uses a simple square, rectangle or circle of fabric, the dimensions of these will be given within the project instructions. The other projects use templates, which are on pages 138–49. These can be traced or photocopied. In some cases, they may need enlarging – this can be easily done with a photocopier or scanner, or even by hand if you are particularly confident! Be sure to cut these templates out with paper-cutting scissors and not your fabric-cutting scissors.

MARKING YOUR FABRIC

There are several ways to transfer your templates and mark your fabric for cutting. Tailor's chalk is convenient because it can be brushed away. Use a white one on dark cloth and a coloured one on lighter fabrics. An air-erasable pen is very easy to use. Most fade after a couple of hours – do check though, as some need washing out. You could also use a pen or a pencil because raw edges will be concealed within seams or hems, so drawn lines will not be visible on the finished project.

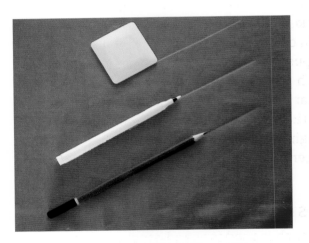

FABRIC STIFFENERS AND STABILIZERS

Fabric stiffeners are available in many weights. An iron-on version reduces the number of layers you're working with once it's fused to a piece of fabric. Use a hot iron to fix the stiffener to the wrong side of the fabric. Read the manufacturer's instructions first, since some stiffeners require steam to fix them firmly. Double-check that your stiffener is glue side down before you press it – cleaning glue off an iron isn't fun.

HAND SEWING

TACKING AND RUNNING STITCH

Tacking is a line of temporary stitches used to fix pieces of fabric in position ready for permanent stitching. Knot the end of the thread and push the needle through from the back of the fabric to the front. Push the needle tip through to the back ³/₈in (1cm) from the place it emerged, then out again to the front of your fabric ³/₈in (1cm) further along. Pull the needle and thread through and repeat. Finish with a couple of stitches worked over each other to secure the end. When the seam or hem has been permanently sewn by machine, remove the tacking. Making your stitch length shorter creates running stitch.

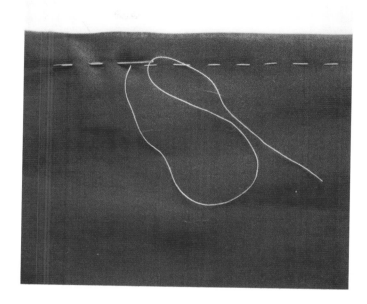

OVERSTITCH

Use overstitch for closing openings for turning. With your two pieces of fabric aligned, or pinned or tacked together, bring up your needle from within one folded edge to the front of your work. Now push your needle through the folded edges of both pieces of fabric and from the back to the front at a slight angle, catching a few threads of fabric from each. Pull the needle and thread through and repeat, spacing your stitches between ¹/₈in (3mm) and ¹/₄in (6mm) apart.

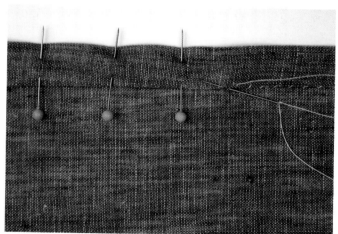

HEM STITCH

This stitch is used for hand-stitching hems and is similar to overstitch. With your hem pinned or tacked, bring your needle up from within the hem's folded edge. Now push your needle through the back layer of fabric, catching a few threads before bringing it through the fold at the top of the hem. Pull the needle and thread through and repeat, spacing your stitches between ¹/₈in (3mm) and ¹/₄in (6mm) apart.

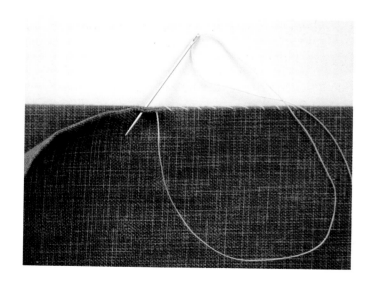

MACHINE SEWING

It is important to keep your machine regularly serviced and covered when not in use. Always refer to your instruction booklet for information specific to your model about changing stitches, reversing, making buttonholes and so on.

Set up the machine where there is plenty of light and you can sit comfortably. Before sewing, make sure that the machine is threaded correctly and that the threads from the needle and bobbin are placed away from you, towards the back of the machine. Turn the wheel towards you so that the needle is in the work, preventing a tangle of threads as you start. Taking it slowly will ensure control of the machine, and problems with the tension or tangling threads will be less likely.

Keep any scraps of the fabric you are working with to test out your machine stitch size and tension before starting on your project. If you have a speed restriction facility on your machine, use this to improve control and accuracy when sewing curves or topstitching.

STRAIGHT STITCH

This stitch is used for all flat seams, hems and topstitching. You can alter the length of straight stitch – when at its longest it can be used for gathering or even tacking.

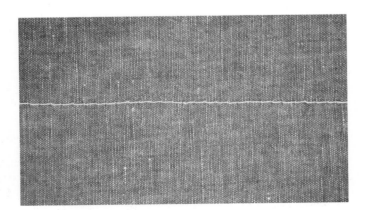

TOPSTITCHING

This is a line of straight machine stitching worked on the right side of the fabric, parallel to seams and edges. It is used as both a functional and a decorative stitch.

ZIGZAG STITCH

Used along raw edges to help reduce fraying, zigzag stitch can also be used to strengthen pressure or stress points. This stitch can be used decoratively and for making buttonholes, too. You can alter the length of the stitches and how close together they are to create different effects. When changing from straight stitch to zigzag, or vice versa, without breaking your stitching, always adjust your stitch with the foot down (to hold your fabric in position) and the needle up.

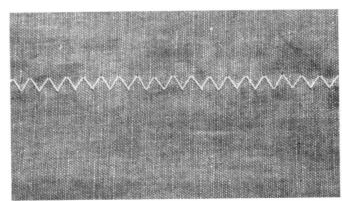

FLAT SEAM

Place the two pieces of fabric together, right sides facing and raw edges aligned. Pin or tack the fabric together. Machine stitch along your sewing line, ³/8in (1cm) from and parallel to the raw edges of the fabrics. Finish the beginning and end of your line of stitching either by hand or by reverse stitching (see page 18).

FRENCH SEAM

A French seam is an efficient way to prevent the raw edges of a seam from fraying. The seam completely encases the raw edges, leaving a neat finish that is ideal for items that get a lot of wear or that are reversible.

1 Place the two pieces of fabric to be joined wrong sides together. Pin or tack before stitching a straight seam along this edge. Trim the seam to ¼in (6mm).

2 Turn your work wrong side out. Tweak and tease the seam with your fingers to make it as neat and sharp as possible. Press the seam and pin or tack along it before stitching a ³/8in (1cm) seam. You will now have encased the raw edges completely within the seam.

3 Give the seam a final press to one side with a hot iron.

REVERSE STITCHING

This is used to reinforce or strengthen a line of stitching, particularly in an area that will be subject to pressure or stress, such as the edges of a turning gap, for example. It can also be used as a quick way to start and end stitching without having to finish off thread ends by hand.

FINISHING OFF THREADS

Finish off thread ends by threading them onto a sewing needle. Then, either make a couple of small, tight stitches before cutting off the thread, or push the needle into a French seam or hem to hide them.

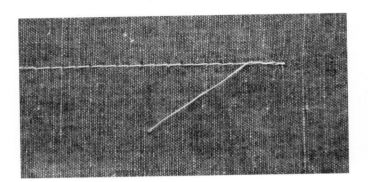

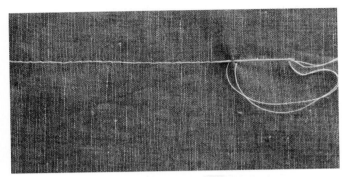

INSERTING A ZIP

Zips need to be inserted accurately so that they work properly and don't catch on the fabric. This is the technique I have found works best.

1 Place the two pieces of fabric right sides together and with the raw edges aligned. Measure and mark with pins where you want to position the zip. Sew a ³⁄₈in (1cm) seam at either side of the zip section, reverse stitching at the pins for extra strength. Now either tack or change your machine to a long stitch and sew a ³⁄₈in (1cm) seam between the two markers.

2 Open out the fabric and press the seam open. With the fabric right side down, lay the zip face down on top of the seam, centred between the markers. Pin or tack all the way around.

3 Turn the fabric over and sew in the zip using a zipper or piping foot on your machine. Sew back and forth a few times as you pass each end of the zip for extra reinforcement. Finally, use a seam ripper to remove the long seam stitches between the two markers.

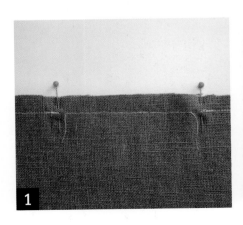

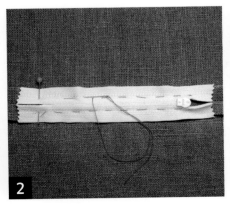

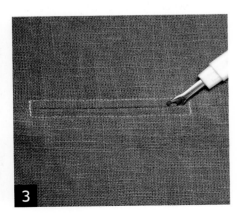

FINISHING TOUCHES

BLANKET STITCH

Used traditionally to hem and decorate the edge of blankets, blanket stitch is also used in embroidery and, with stitches sewn close together, to edge buttonholes.

1 Imagine two parallel stitch lines roughly ¼in (6mm) apart. Bring the thread through to the front of your work on the top line. Insert the needle ¼in (6mm) further along on the bottom line and through to the front again parallel to where it was inserted, at the same time keeping the working thread under the needle point.

2 Pull your thread through and to the right to form an 'L' shape.

3 Reinsert the needle ¼in (6mm) further along in the bottom line and through to the front again parallel to where it was inserted before, keeping the working thread under the needle. Pull your needle and thread through and to the right again. Continue in this way to make a line of blanket stitch.

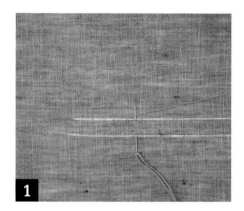

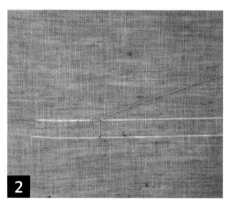

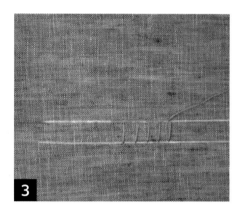

TRIMMING CORNERS AND CURVES

Corners should be cut across at an angle so they are sharp when the work is turned right side out (A). On curved seams, cut 'V' shapes into the seam close to the stitch line to make the seam smooth when the work is turned right side out (B). Snip very carefully with small, sharp scissors to avoid cutting through the seam line by mistake.

PRESSING SEAMS

Have all the equipment for ironing set up ready to use, close to where you are working. Press each seam as you complete it. Your iron should have adjustable heat settings and a steam option. Use the point of the iron to open seams. Steam produces the right amount of moisture to make a crisp edge and flat seam, but steam scalds easily so be careful not to hurt your fingers. The project instructions will tell you whether to press a seam to one side or to press it open.

BUTTONHOLES

Use this method to ensure your buttonholes are a perfect fit for the buttons you have chosen.

1 Using your chosen button as a size guide, mark the position for your button on the fabric – the diameter of your button dictates the length of your buttonhole. For horizontal buttonholes, the position of the button should be near the end closest to the opening. For vertical buttonholes, it should be central. Use small, sharp scissors to cut along the length of your buttonhole.

2 Press the fabric with a hot iron. Using sewing thread, make a line of small running stitches (see page 15) around the buttonhole line – this helps to reduce fraying and holds layers of fabric together if you are working through several thicknesses. Then cut the buttonhole.

3 Starting at one end of the buttonhole, make very close buttonhole stitches (blanket stitch; see page 19) all around the opening, about 1/8in (3mm) long.

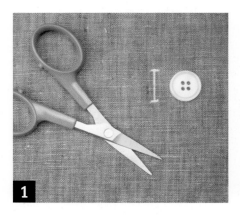

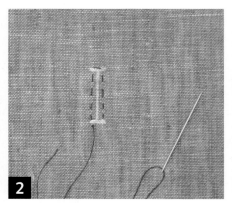

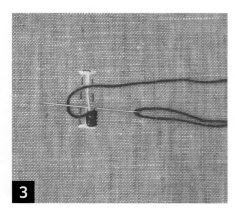

BUTTON LOOP

Hand-made button loops are very satisfying to make and add a cute delicacy to a project. The loops take up a surprising amount of thread, and running out halfway causes difficulties.

1 Sew on the button. Use pins to mark the position of the loop. Push your threaded needle up through the fabric's folded edge at the point of the left-hand pin, leaving the knotted end within the fold. Push the needle back in at the point of the right-hand pin, and out again by the left-hand pin. Pull the needle to leave a loop of thread wide enough to go over your button. Repeat until the loop has four strands.

2 Remove the pins. Starting at the right-hand side, sew buttonhole stitches (blanket stitch; see page 19) over all the strands and the loose thread until you reach the left-hand side. Fasten off securely with a few small, tight stitches.

3 Your button should fit neatly into the loop.

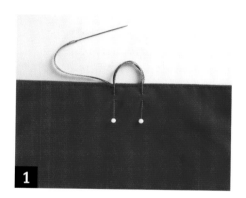

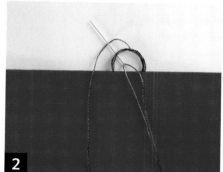

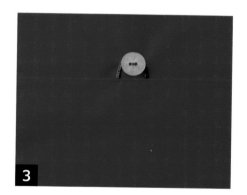

HANGING LOOP

This is a narrow tube of fabric that can be used for hanging your work. Take a piece of fabric of the required length and 1½in (4cm) wide (unless otherwise stated). Fold each long edge in by ³⁄₈in (1cm) to meet in the centre and press. Fold again so that the folded edges meet then pin or tack. Topstitch ¹⁄₈in (3mm) in from both long edges.

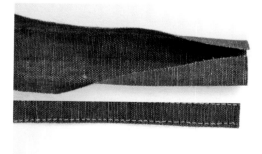

SEWING ON BUTTONS

With your thread doubled and knotted at the end, pull the needle through to the front of the fabric. Sew the button on securely through the holes, then pull the needle through so that the thread lies between the button and the fabric. Wind the thread around the stitches, take the needle through to the back of the fabric and finish off.

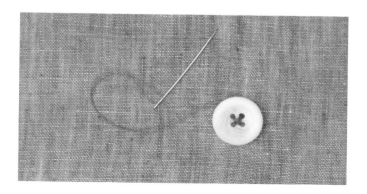

MAKING DRAWSTRINGS

You can use twisted cords as drawstrings, but making your own in fabric is very satisfying and looks great.

1 Cut a strip of fabric 1½in (4cm) wide and about 2in (5cm) more than your required finished length. Lay a piece of string, at least 6in (15cm) longer than your fabric, along the length of the right side of the strip. Align one end of the string at one short end and zigzag stitch it very firmly in place.

2 Fold the strip of fabric in half to align the long, raw edges and encase the string within it. Stitch a seam, using a zipper foot if available, along the length of the fabric strip through the centre of it, ³⁄₈in (1cm) from the raw edges. Ensure that the string is lying snug within the fold and does not get snagged in the stitch line. Trim the seam allowance down to ³⁄₁₆in (5mm).

3 Now turn the tube of fabric right side out. This is done by drawing it out through one open end, carefully yet firmly pulling the tail end of the string. This is difficult to start with, but becomes easier once you get going. You may have to kick start the process by poking the zigzag-stitched end of the string down into the tube with a blunt tool such as the end of a knitting needle.

4 Snip off the string attached to one end and give your drawstring a press with a hot iron.

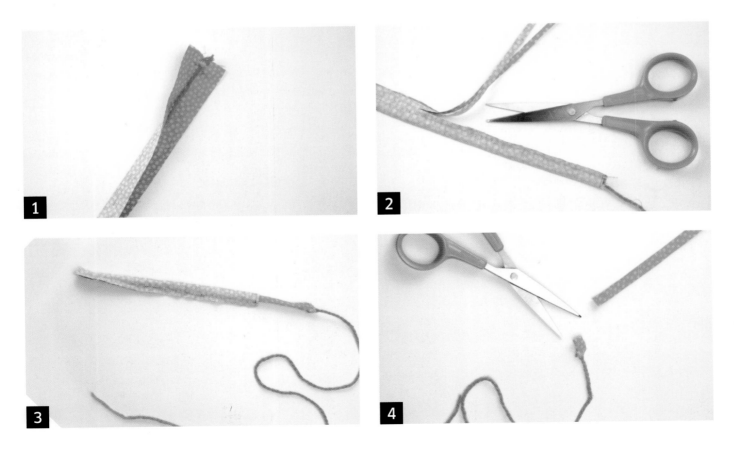

1

2

3

4

MAKING YO-YOS

A yo-yo maker is a great tool for turning scraps of fabric into embellishments to revamp soft furnishings or garments.

1 With your fabric right side down on the outer half of the yo-yo maker, clip the inner half on top and cut out a circle using the outside of the maker as a guide.

2 With the thread doubled, stitch around the fabric using the guide holes in the yo-yo maker to create a tacked hem around the edge of your circle of fabric.

3 With your needle and thread still attached, separate the outer and inner parts of the yo-yo maker and gently ease the fabric away from them.

4 Draw your needle and thread to gather the edges of the circle of fabric into the centre.

5 Make a few small stitches on top of each other to hold the gathering in place and finish it off.

If you do not have a yo-yo maker, cut circles of fabric 3½in (9cm) in diameter. Fold in the raw edges by ½in (1.25cm) and tack with regular sized stitches, ⅛in (3mm) in from the folded edge. Use doubled thread for strength. Draw the thread tight, gathering the outside edge of your circle into the centre, and finish off the thread securely by overstitching several times (see page 15).

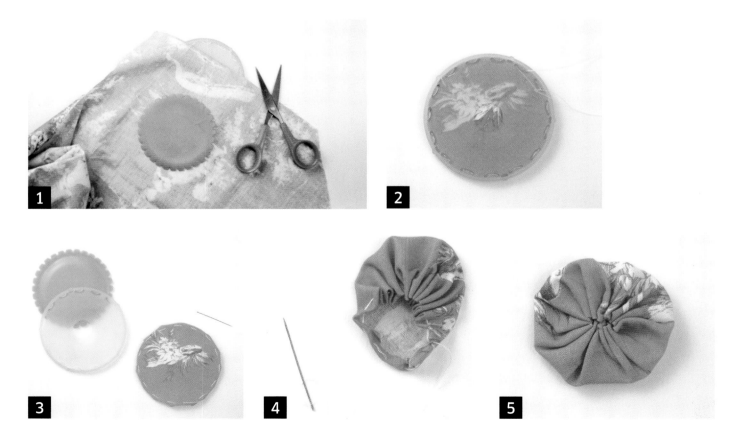

ADDITIONAL TECHNIQUES

TURNING GAPS

Turning gaps are wonderful! They enable you to make seemingly invisible joins between outer fabrics and their linings. Usually hidden inside bags or sacks, turning gaps are great for producing a really smart finish to projects.

1 When sewing the lining of a bag, leave a gap of about 4in (10cm) or more in your line of stitching along one edge. It's wise to reverse stitch as you stop sewing at either side of the gap to avoid tearing the seam when you pull your work right side out through it.

2 Press open the seam where the turning gap is located – this will help when you are hand stitching it closed. Turn your work right side out by pulling it through the turning gap. Tweak and tease all your seams and corners to make them sharp and neat, and give them a good press with a hot iron. Fold in the raw edges around the gap and pin. Close the gap by hand sewing with overstitch (see page 15).

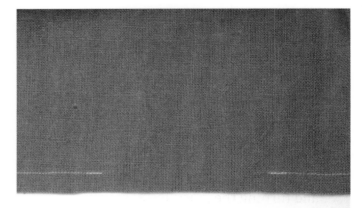

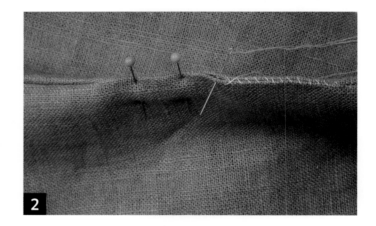

JOINING TRIMS

To join the two raw ends of a trim, fold them at 45 degrees away from the seam line and over the raw edge of the fabric, so that the ends are 'lost' within the seam allowance.

BOX CORNERS

Box corners give body to a bag or cushion and can create a very professional-looking finish.

1 Place two pieces of fabric right sides together. Align the raw edges and pin or tack them together. Using a straight stitch, sew the side and bottom seams. Pivot at the corners by leaving the needle down, raising the machine's foot and turning the fabric by 90 degrees.

2 Press the seams open. With the sewn fabric still right sides together, match the side seam with the bottom fold (or seam) to create a point at one corner. Pin to hold the seams together. It is very important to match the seams perfectly; this will make your finished corner look smart.

3 Mark the line of the box corner with a pen or tailor's chalk. Sew across the drawn line several times, reverse stitching at the beginning and end for strength. Leaving a ³⁄₈in (1cm) seam allowance, cut the triangular point off the corner.

4 Turn your work right side out and press neatly. Repeat this process with the other corner.

BINDING STRAIGHT EDGES

Use tape, bias binding or strips of fabric to bind straight raw edges. As long as your edges are straight and you are making mitres at the corners (see page opposite) you do not need to use strips of fabric cut on the bias, although shop-bought bias binding is very easy to use.

1 Cut the binding to the length of the outer edge of your work, plus at least 1in (2.5cm). Place it on the work right sides together and so that one edge aligns with the raw fabric edge. Pin or tack in position then machine stitch slowly and carefully along the binding fold crease.

2 Turn your work over. Fold the binding down to meet the stitch line so that it encases the raw edge of your work. Sew down by hand with hem stitch (see page 15).

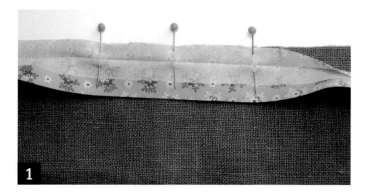

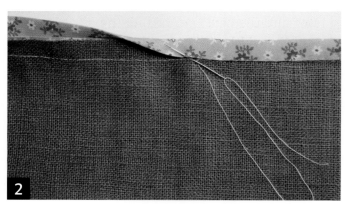

BINDING CURVED EDGES

Curved edges require binding with fabric cut on the bias to avoid excessive puckering. The easiest way to do this is to use pre-made bias binding.

1 Open out the binding. Place it on your work right sides together and position the upper fold along your stitch line. Encourage the binding to follow the fabric curves. Pin or tack in place and stitch slowly and carefully along the fold crease.

2 Turn your work over. Fold the binding down to meet the stitch line so that it encases the raw edge of your work. Sew down by hand with hem stitch (see page 15).

3 Turn your work back over again and give it a good press with a hot iron.

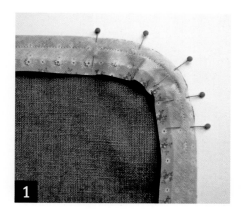

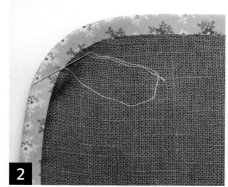

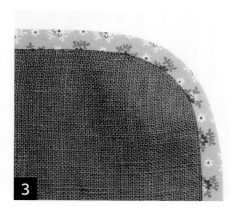

MITRE CORNERS

Mitre corners are crisp and sharp, and well worth the effort for binding tablecloths and quilts. Use binding that measures twice the final width you want; for a ½in (1.25cm) bound border, use 1in (2.5cm)-wide binding (plus seam allowance if you are not using bias binding). In terms of length, you need enough binding to cover your seams, plus 3in (7.5cm) for finishing off.

1 Measure the width of the binding. Draw a line half the width of the binding in from the raw edges to be bound. Starting halfway along one edge, open out the binding and lay it right side down so that its bottom fold crease lies on your pencil line. Machine stitch along the crease of the binding until you reach the corner turn of the pencil line. Remove your work from the machine and finish off the thread ends by hand.

2 Fold your binding back over itself and upwards at 90 degrees.

3 Fold the binding back down over itself at 180 degrees so that the mitre point lies exactly over the corner point of the fabric. Pin or tack the binding along the next edge so that its bottom fold crease lies on your pencil line. Reinsert the machine needle where your last stitching finished, in the corner fold. Turn the wheel by hand to place it accurately, and stitch along the crease of the binding to the next corner. Repeat the process all the way around the work.

4 Turn your work over. Fold the binding down to encase the raw seam edge. Pin or tack in position before sewing all the way around by hand using hem stitch (see page 15).

5 Take your time at each corner to fold a neat mitre, mirroring those on the other side.

6 Press the binding from both sides to neaten any uneven corners.

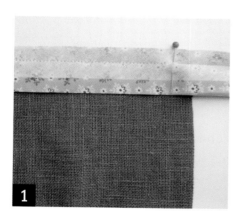

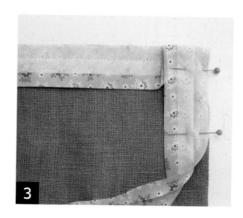
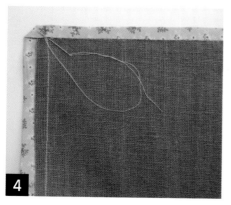
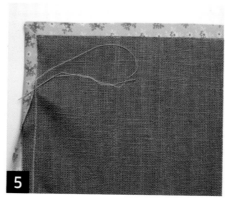

IN THE KITCHEN

CHILD'S APRON

A perfect cover-up for those cooking or painting days, this is a fairly easy and quick project that can be made out of most middle- to heavyweight fabrics. Use another scrap of fabric to add a pocket, or make a smaller version for a toy (see page 32).

Find the template on page 144

You will need
1 fat quarter of cotton fabric
68½in (174cm) of 1in (2.5cm)-wide cotton webbing or tape
Tracing paper or baking parchment
Pencil
Scissors
Sewing machine
Thread to match fabric
Pins
Dress-making scissors
Sewing needle
Iron

NOTE: You can make a larger apron by using two continuous fat quarters and resizing the pattern accordingly.

1 Make the template by enlarging the one on page 144. Fold the fabric in half along its longest side. Use the template to cut the fabric, ensuring the 'fold' edge lies along the fold in the fabric. Open out your fabric piece and lay it right side down. Fold the two curved edges in by ³⁄₈in (1cm) and tack in position. Press with a hot iron.

2 Fold both curved edges in again by ³⁄₈in (1cm) and pin or tack down. Use your machine to stitch these two curved hems along the edges.

3 Create a hem along the bottom edge of the apron in exactly the same way, folding in the raw edge by ³⁄₈in (1cm), then ³⁄₈in (1cm) again. Tack or pin the seam before stitching it by machine.

4 Cut two 24in (60cm) lengths from the tape to make the waist ties. Fold one end of each one over twice and stitch down by hand or machine to prevent the end of the ties from fraying.

5 Lay the apron right side down in front of you, with the bottom hem nearest you. Take one of the tape ties and lay it across the fabric from left to right, with the left-hand edge butting up to the raw left-hand edge of the apron and snug up against the bottom of the curved hem. Pin in position.

6 Fold the raw left-hand edge of the apron in by ³⁄₈in (1cm) and then fold by another ³⁄₈in (1cm) to form a hem. Pin or tack in position.

7 Use your machine to stitch a neat hem, taking care when sewing over the pins holding the tape. Now fold the strip of tape to the left, and pin it down onto the hem you've just sewn.

8 Sew across the width of the tape several times by machine to secure it firmly. Repeat these steps to attach the second tie to the right-hand edge of the apron. Following this method, attach the remaining 20½in (52cm) strip of tape to the top edge of the apron to form the neckband.

Tip

When you are stitching the curved hems, make sure you work slowly – use the speed control if your machine has this function. Taking your time is far better than having to unpick the seam if you go slightly off course.

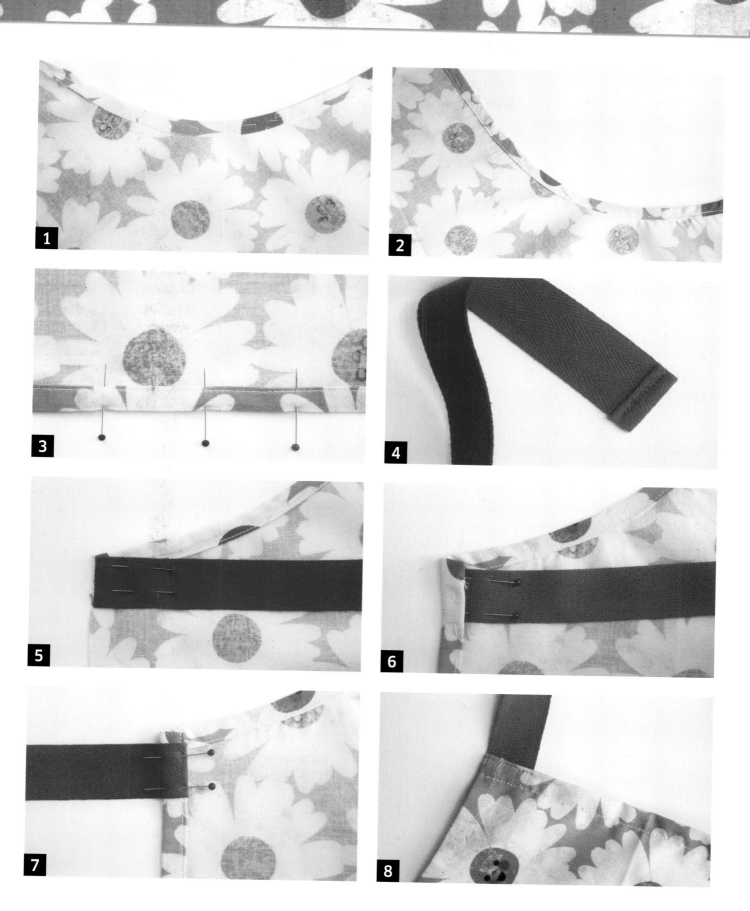

POT HANDLE SLEEVES

This is a great gift for a chef. Pans that work on the hob and in the oven are lovely, but you need good pot holders while handling them. These practical, padded sleeves will protect you from burns and add a splash of colour to the kitchen at the same time.

Find the template on page 140

You will need
½ fat quarter of outer fabric
½ fat quarter of lining fabric
15 x 9½in (36 x 24cm) of wadding
7in (18cm) length of ¾in (2cm)-wide bias binding
Tape measure or ruler
Sewing machine
Thread to match fabric
Sewing needle
Pins
Dress-making scissors
Pen or fabric marker
Iron
Knitting needle or other blunt tool for pushing out corners

NOTE: You can make the whole project from the same fabric – one fat quarter will make two sleeves.

Tip
This is a great project for using up scraps – the outer fabric could be patched from small leftover pieces.

1 Use the template on page 140 to cut out the outer fabric, lining and wadding. Prepare the hanging loop first (see page 21). Fold the bias binding in half, wrong sides facing. Topstitch by machine just in from the edge, along the length of the fabric (see page 16).

2 Lay down your lining fabric, right side up. Place your outer fabric on top of it, right side down, and the wadding on top of that. Align all the raw edges.

3 Pin or tack along one short end through all three layers of fabric and then stitch a $3/8$in (1cm) seam by machine along this edge.

4 Open out your work so that the lining lies on its own to one side, the wadding and outer fabrics on the other. Press the seam away from the lining with a hot iron so that it lies against the wadding. Pin or tack along the seam allowance through all layers of fabric.

5 Topstitch through the seam allowance $3/16$in (5mm) from the seam stitching. When you turn your work over, you should have a neat line of stitching $3/16$in (5mm) within the edge of the outer fabric, anchoring it to the wadding.

6 Take your prepared bias binding and fold it in half to form a loop. Place the right side of your work facing you, the outer fabric on the right and lying horizontally. Position the loop's folded end to the left, with the raw ends $3/8$in (1cm) from the right-hand edge of your work. Place it $1 1/2$in (4cm) above the bottom right-hand corner. Pin or tack it in place.

7 Fold your work in half lengthways, right sides facing, and align all the edges before pinning. Now re-cut your template along the stitch line indicated. Place the template along the fold where indicated and draw around it.

8 Sew by machine along your marked stitch line, starting and finishing either side of the marked Xs on the template on the lining only, leavin the turning gap open. Reverse stitch at each side of these marks for strength.

9 Trim your seam allowance all the way around your stitch line to $3/16$in (5mm), apart from at the turning gap, where you should leave a $3/8$in (1cm) seam allowance.

10 Turn your work right sides out through the turning gap. Use the end of a knitting needle, or another blunt tool, to prod out the ends from the inside.

11 At the turning gap, tuck in the raw edges. Press and close it by hand using overstitch (see page 15).

12 Tweak and manipulate the seam around the padded outer end of your work to make it as sharp and neat as you can before pressing it with a hot iron. Now push the lining down inside the outer fabric, using the end of the knitting needle to ensure it fits snugly right to the very end. Give the whole padded sleeve a final press.

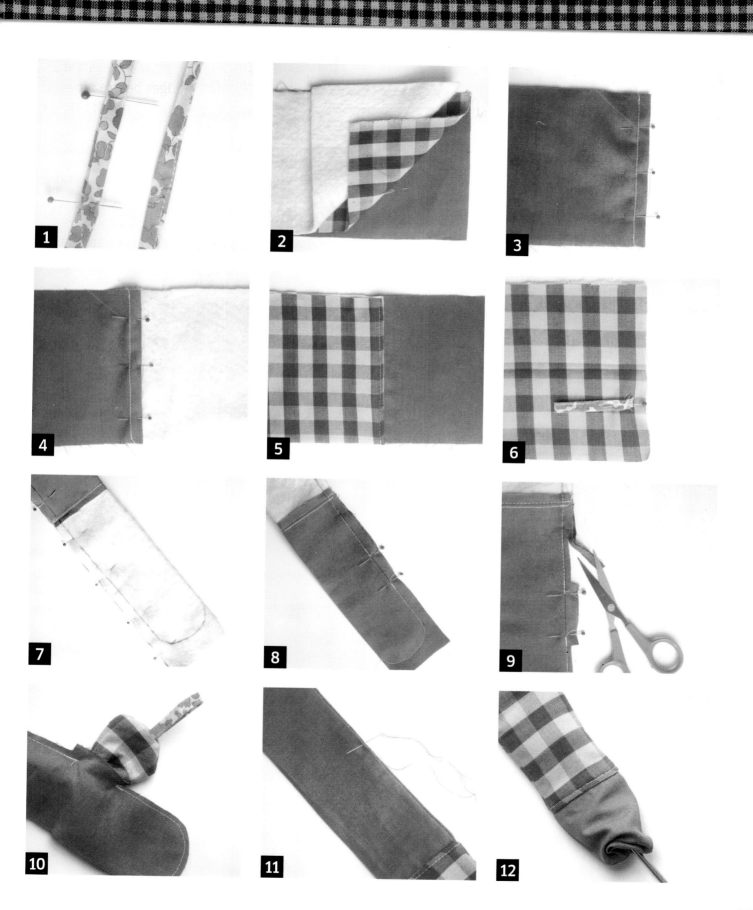

PATCHWORK COASTERS

Coasters are the perfect project for using up little fabric scraps. They can be given as sets of four, but they needn't all match. Stack them up and tie a contrasting ribbon around them with a label for a very satisfying homemade gift indeed.

Find the templates on page 141

You will need

Various scraps of patterned and plain fabrics – see the templates
    for patch sizes
4in (10cm) square of very heavy stabilizer
4in (10cm) square of backing fabric
18in (45.5cm) of ¾in (2cm)-wide bias binding
Tracing paper or baking parchment
Pencil
Scissors
Tape measure or ruler
Sewing machine
Thread to match fabric
Sewing needle
Pins
Dress-making scissors
Pen or fabric marker
Iron

NOTE: One fat quarter will make seven plain coasters. Start at step 5 if you are using the same fabric throughout the project.

1 Cut two pieces of fabric using template A on page 141. Place the two pieces right sides together, aligning the edges, and pin or tack along one short edge.

2 Stitch a ³/₈in (1cm) seam by machine along the pinned edge. Press the seam open with a hot iron.

3 Place the joined pieces of fabric right side up in front of you. Cut a piece of fabric using template B (see page 141) and place it right side down on top, aligning all the raw edges. Pin or tack along the longest edge.

4 Stitch a ³/₈in (1cm) seam along your pinned edge and press it open with a hot iron.

5 Place the backing fabric right side down in front of you. Put the stabilizer on top, and finally your pieced fabric, right side up.

6 Align all the raw edges and trim where necessary. Turn your work over. Tack through all the layers all the way around to hold the fabrics firmly in position.

7 Turn over your 'sandwich' of fabrics. Open out the bias binding, right side down, and turn in the short end in by ³/₁₆in (5mm). Starting in the middle of one edge, pin the binding to the coaster, aligning its top raw edge with the edge of your coaster. Pin the binding in place to the next corner.

8 Follow the instructions for binding straight edges and creating mitre corners on pages 26 and 27, and bind around the edges of the coaster. When you reach the edge where you started, trim your binding to overlap the initial folded end by ³/₁₆–³/₈in (5–10mm). Sew along from the corner to the end of the binding.

9 Turn your work over. Fold the bias binding over to encase the raw edges of the coaster. Pin or tack it in position before sewing it down by hand using hem stitch (see page 15). Carefully fold and manipulate the binding at each corner to create neat mitres.

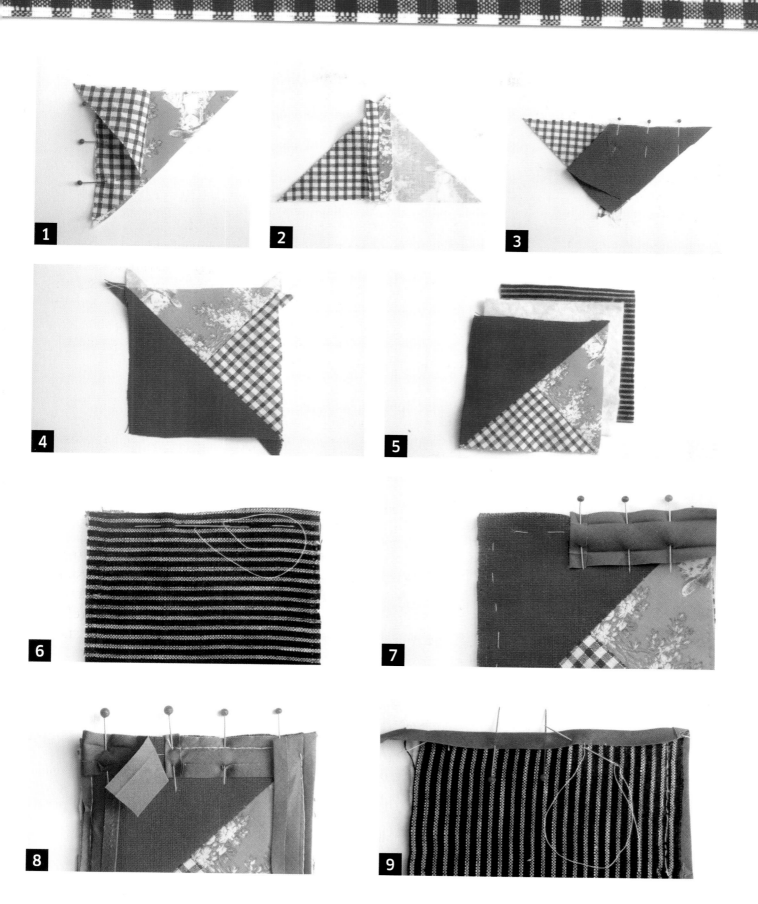

PLATE DIVIDERS

These very practical makes stop delicate, heavy or precious plates from being chipped, scratched or broken so that they can enjoy a longer life. You can use any variety of fabrics and any trim — why not try lace or pompoms instead of rickrack?

You will need
2 circles of fabric the size of your plate plus 1in (2.5cm)
Trim to fit the circumference of the fabric circles (this will leave just enough for joining the trim when you stitch it down)
Tape measure or ruler
Sewing machine
Thread to match fabric
Sewing needle
Pins
Dress-making scissors
Pen or fabric marker
Iron

NOTE: The plate dividers can be made any size, as long as your fabric circles measure 1in (2.5cm) wider than the diameter of the plates. To fit a standard average dinner plate size of 12in (30cm), you will need two fat quarters of fabric so that you can cut two circles of 13¾in (32.5cm) diameter.

1 Place one of the circles of fabric right side facing you. Pin and then tack the trim around the edge of the fabric, ensuring that the stitching lies exactly where the seam should be sewn, ³/8in (1cm) in from the raw edge. Fold the leading edge of your trim forwards and upwards so that it will be lost within the seam allowance.

2 Once the trim is tacked around the complete circumference, mark a 3in (7.5cm) turning gap (away from the join of the trim ends) and mark either side of it with pins. Machine sew the trim to your fabric between these two pins.

3 Place the two circles of fabric right sides together. Align their edges and pin or tack them around the edge. If you tack, use a different colour thread to the one used in step 1, so that you know which one to follow when stitching your seam. Make sure you have marked either side of your turning gap so that you know exactly where it is and don't stitch across it by accident.

4 Stitch a seam around the circumference of your work by machine, starting at one side of your turning gap and finishing at the other – reverse stitch as you start and finish (see page 18). Stitch with the piece of fabric with the trim tacked to it on top and follow your original tacking as your stitch line. Remove the tacking. Turn the work right sides out through the turning gap. There is no need to snip the edges because the curve is very gentle on a circle this size.

5 Tease and manipulate the seam all around your work to make it as crisp and sharp as possible and give it a good press with a hot iron. Turn in the raw edges of the turning gap and pin or tack in position.

6 Close the turning gap neatly with overstitch (see page 15).

7 Sew a line of topstitching (see page 16) by machine, ³/16in (5mm) in from the edge all the way around, and finish off your thread ends (see page 18).

Tip

If you are making these plate dividers for someone who has particularly delicate plates, you could add wadding in step 3 for extra protection.

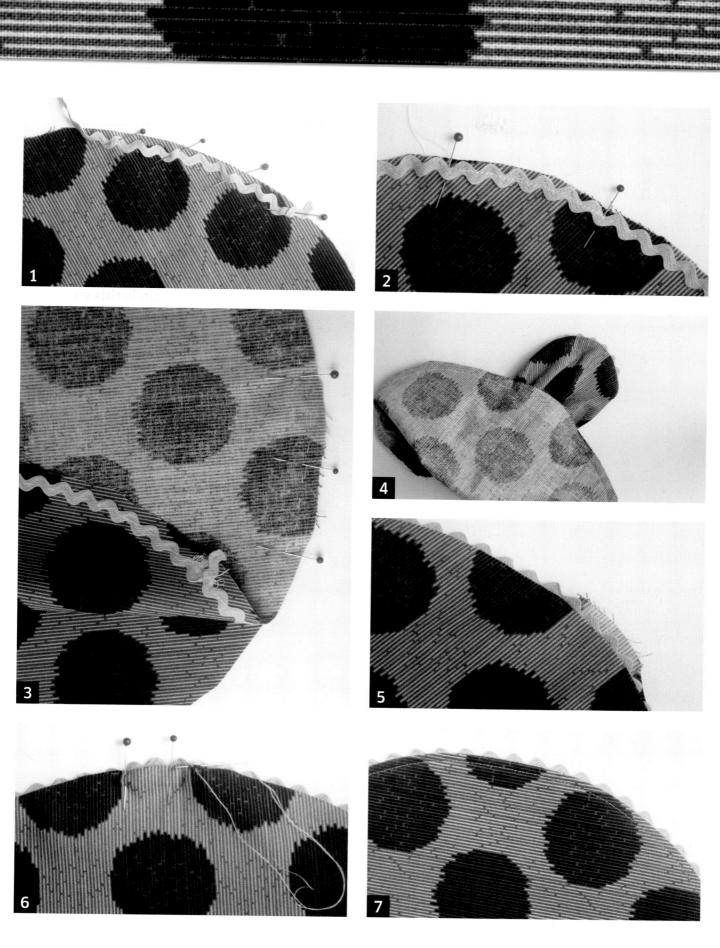

TOPKNOT EGG COSY

Perfect for Easter, or a special breakfast on Mother's Day, these cute padded egg cosies use very little fabric and are great when given as a half-dozen set. Choose your fabric to reflect the occasion and start a special day with a boiled egg.

Find the template on page 141

You will need
10 x 4in (25 x 10cm) of outer fabric
10 x 4in (25 x 10cm) of wadding
4 x 1½in (10 x 4cm) of contrasting fabric for the topknot
8in (20cm) string
Tape measure or ruler
Tracing paper or baking parchment
Pencil
Scissors
Sewing machine and thread
Needle and thread
Pins
Dress-making scissors
Pen or fabric marker
Iron

NOTE: One fat quarter will make six egg cosies – you will still need to use contrasting stash fabrics for the topknots.

1 Use the template on page 141 to cut out four pieces of wadding. Lay two pieces on top of one another so that all the edges align. Pin or tack along one edge and sew a ³/₈in (1cm) seam along one curved edge, stopping ³/₈in (1cm) before the centre top point (marked 'A' on the template). Reverse stitch (see page 18) at the start and finish. Repeat this with the other two pieces of wadding.

2 Trim the seam allowance down to just ¹/₈in (3mm) on both stitched pairs of wadding.

3 Open out your two pieces of work and place them right sides together. Align the curved edges. Pin or tack them together carefully and then stitch a ³/₈in (1cm) seam all along this edge, passing across point A, and reverse stitching as you start and finish.

4 Trim the seam allowance on this long curved seam down to ¹/₈in (3mm).

5 Cut four pieces of outer fabric using the same template. Follow step 1 so that you have two stitched pairs of outer fabric pieces. Do not trim.

6 Carefully press the two seams with a hot iron, taking care not to burn your fingers. Place one piece right side up in front of you. Make a length of drawstring (see page 22) with your contrasting fabric. Tie a knot in one end and place it on the central seam on the right side of one of the pieces, at point A, so that 1¹/₄in (3cm) of the un knotted end protrudes over and above the top edge of the fabric. Pin and tack it in position.

7 Place the second piece of outer fabric face down on top of the first one. Align all the curved edges and pin or tack around them.

8 Sew a ³/₈in (1cm) seam all the way around the curved edge, reverse stitching at the beginning and end, and when passing over the topknot. Trim the excess topknot fabric flush with the seam's raw edge.

9 Press this last seam open as best you can, again being very careful of your fingers. Turn the outer fabric right sides out and slot the wadding piece into it, still inside out. Push it in so that it's a snug fit.

10 Trim the wadding that falls below the bottom raw edge of the outer fabric. Make a line of tacking ³/₄in (2cm) from the bottom raw edge through both the outer fabric and the wadding around the circumference of your work to anchor the two layers together. Now trim the wadding so that it is ⁵/₈in (1.5cm) shorter than the outer fabric – it may be easiest to do this with the work turned inside out.

11 Turn the work inside out if you haven't done so already, and fold up the raw edge of the outer fabric to meet the bottom of the wadding. Fold it up once more to form a neat hem – the bottom edge of the wadding should sit snugly in the second fold of the hem. Pin or tack all the way around. Sew the hem by hand using hem stitch (see page 15) – try to catch the fold of the hem and the wadding only, not the outer layer of fabric.

12 Turn your work right side out and give it a press with a hot iron.

Tip

Consider customizing your design by adding a tassel or a pompom in place of the topknot.

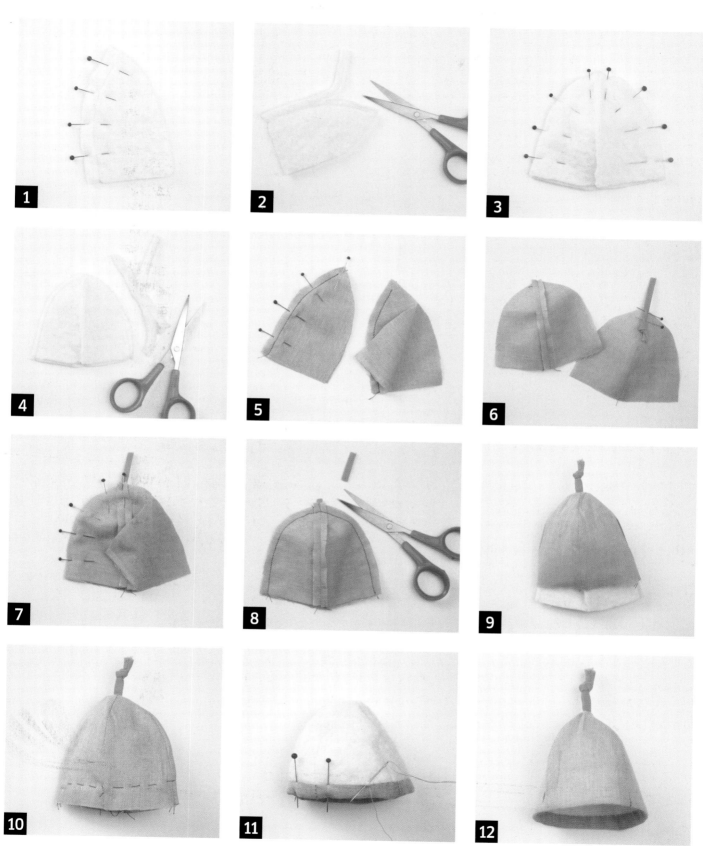

IN THE OFFICE

HANGING POCKETS

This is a handy space saver for the office. Using stabilizer gives this project form and solidity, and each pocket could be made from a different scrap of fabric. If you have more fabric, make the backing panel longer and add more pockets.

Find the templates on page 147

You will need

1½ fat quarters each of two different fabrics: cut one 15¾ x 10in (40 x 25cm) rectangle in each fabric for the backing panel; the rest will be used for the pockets

33¼ x 14in (88 x 36cm) of stabilizer: cut one 15¾ x 10in (40 x 25cm) rectangle for the backing panel; the rest is for the pockets

95in (241cm) of ¾in (2cm)-wide binding: 55in (140cm) for the backing panel, 28in (71cm) for the pockets, 12in (30cm) for the hanging loops

Tracing paper or greaseproof paper

Pencil

Scissors

Tape measure or ruler

Sewing machine

Thread to match fabric

Zipper foot

Needle and thread

Pins

Dress-making scissors

Pen or fabric marker

Iron

Clips for holding fabric together

NOTE: You can make the whole project from the same fabric – you will need three fat quarters of material.

Tip

You could rescale the templates to make narrower pockets for pens and pencils.

1 Use the templates on page 147 to cut out the pocket pieces from the outer fabric, lining and stabilizer. Place one pocket front and one pocket lining piece right sides together, with the lining fabric at the front. Align the raw edges and pin or tack along the bottom edge. Sew a ³/₈in (1cm) seam along this edge and press open. With the work still wrong side up, place a piece of stabilizer centrally above the seam, with its top, angled edge aligned with the top edge of the pocket front. There should be a ³/₈in (1cm) gap between the seam and the bottom of the stabilizer.

2 Fold the lining up over the stabilizer, aligning the top edge. Press with a hot iron to fuse. Turn your work over and iron the pocket front to fuse it to the stabilizer.

3 Open out the bias binding and lay it face down along the front top edge of the pocket piece. Align and pin or tack before stitching a ³/₈in (1cm) seam along this edge.

4 Turn your work over and fold the binding over twice. Pin before hand sewing with hem stitch (see page 15). Trim the binding flush with the edge of the pocket piece. Repeat steps 1–4 to complete the second pocket.

5 Place the back fabric right side down. Place the stabilizer on top of it and the front fabric on top, right side up. Use a hot iron to fuse the stabilizer by ironing it on both sides.

6 Lay the backing piece right side up, with one short edge nearest to you. Place a pocket piece on top, right side up and 4in (10cm) above the bottom edge. Pin in place before stitching by machine ¼in (6mm) above the bottom edge of the pocket.

7 Place the second pocket piece on top, overlapping the first pocket and with its bottom ½in (1.25cm) above the bottom edge of the backing piece. Pin in place and machine stitch ¼in (6mm) above its bottom edge.

8 Stitch down the right-hand sides of the pockets. Push the stabilized central part of the pocket pieces to the left and firmly pin the two layers of each pocket piece so that they align exactly with the edge of the backing piece. Use the zipper foot to make a line of stitching ³/₈in (1cm) from the edge. Reverse stitch over the bound edges of the pockets for extra strength (see page 18).

9 Trim the edge of your work flush with the bottom pocket. Trim the sides evenly too.

10 Turn over your work and mark two points, each 2in (5cm) in from the corners of the top edge. Make two 6in (15cm)-long hanging loops. Fold the two loops in half and pin the marked point; the loops should hang inwards and the raw ends protrude just over the edge. Stitch by machine back and forth over the loops, ³/₈in (1cm) in from the edge of the backing panel. Cut the raw ends of the loops flush with the edge of your work.

11 Make your starting point about 6in (15cm) from the bottom edge and make a neat mitre at each corner (see page 27). Place the open binding right side down on the front of your work and follow the instructions for binding straight edges (see page 26).

12 Turn over and fold the binding over twice before stitching it down by hand using hem stitch (see page 15). Take care at the corners to make neat, sharp mitres.

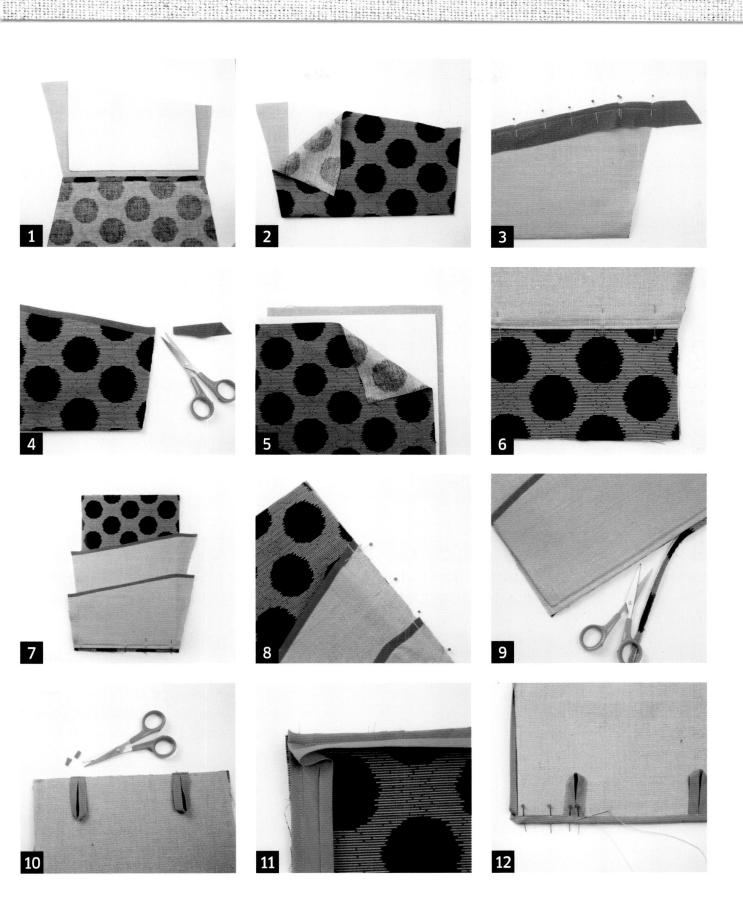

PENCIL CASE

This is a well-proportioned pencil case with a wide opening so that you can easily find just what you need. You could make it with a water-resistant fabric lining so it is suitable for make-up or small paintbrushes, or create a larger version for travel essentials.

Find the templates on page 143

You will need
½ fat quarter of outer fabric
½ fat quarter of lining fabric
10in (25cm) zip
Tracing paper or greaseproof paper
Pencil
Scissors
Tape measure or ruler
Sewing machine and thread
Zipper foot
Needle and thread
Pins
Dress-making scissors
Pen or fabric marker
Iron

NOTE: One fat quarter will make one pencil case if you use the same material for the lining.

1 Cut out two pieces of outer fabric using template A, and one piece of lining fabric cut on the fold using template B (see page 143). Place the two pieces of outer fabric right sides together with the edges aligned. Pin or tack a seam on either side from points 'a' and 'b', indicated on the template. Sew a ³/8in (1cm) seam along the two sides, reverse stitching at both ends (see page 18). Press open the seams with a hot iron – be careful not to burn your fingertips.

2 With your work still wrong side out, fold over the two top curved edges to the wrong side of your work by ³/8in (1cm). Pin and then tack along these edges, making the curves on the folds as smooth as you can.

3 Carefully tack the zip in position along the curved edge. Do this with your work right side out – as you are attaching the zip to a curved edge, it's far better to tack than simply pin. Butt the folded edge of the fabric to the outside edge of the zip teeth along either side.

4 With the zip open, topstitch (see page 16) by machine with a zipper foot all the way around the zip, ¹/8–³/16in (3–5mm) from the edge. This is quite a fiddly process, so take it very slowly.

5 Turn your work wrong side out and, with the zip at least one-third open, align the two bottom edges and pin or tack them in position before machine stitching a ³/8in (1cm) seam.

6 Fold the lining fabric right sides together. Pin or tack a seam on either side from points 'a' and 'b', as indicated on the template. Sew a ³/8in (1cm) seam along the two sides, reverse stitching at either end for extra strength.

7 Press open the seams with a hot iron. Repeat step 2 with the lining fabric.

8 Turn the lining piece right side out and the outer fabric wrong side out. Slot the outer fabric piece inside the lining and pin or tack the top folded edge neatly around the wrong side of the zip. Use small hem stitching (see page 15) to attach the lining all around the zip as neatly as you can.

9 Turn your work right side out again through the zip. Using your fingers, tweak and prod from the inside of each of the two corners to make the lining fit snugly within the outer fabric corners. Flatten the corners, aligning the side seams with the outer bottom seam, and give them a good press with a hot iron.

10 Use the box corner template to mark your stitch line. Pin or tack before sewing by machine. Trim off the corner point ³/16in (5mm) from the stitch line.

11 Turn the work inside out again and tweak and manipulate the two box corner seams to make them as sharp as possible. Press with a hot iron and pin or tack in position. Sew a ³/8in (1cm) seam along this edge to create both a French seam (see page 17) and a box corner (see page 25).

12 Turn your work right side out and give it a good press with a hot iron.

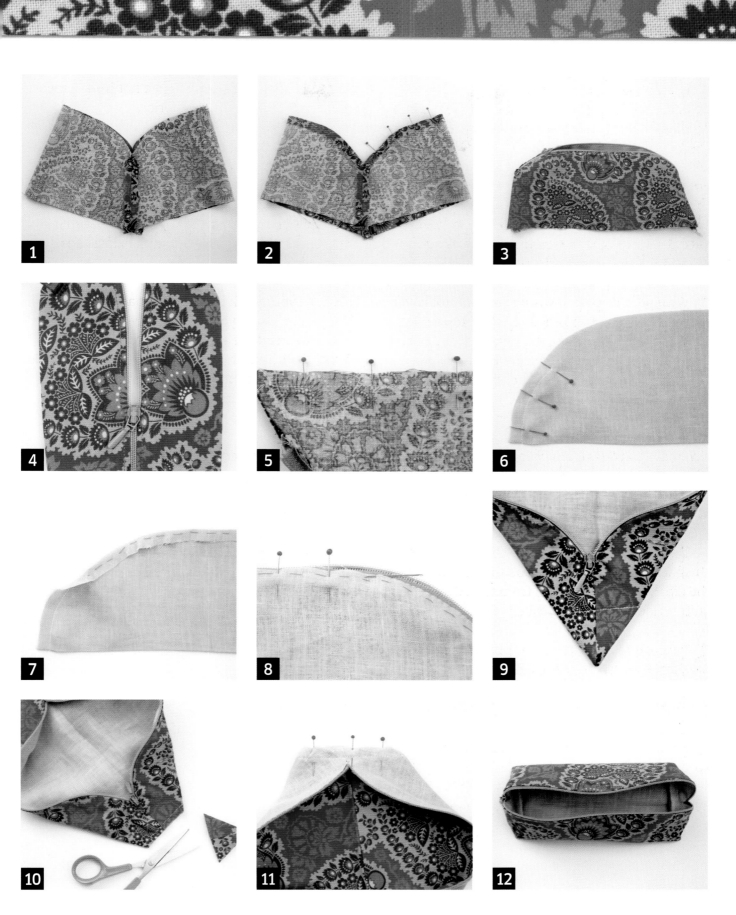

GLASSES POUCH

Protect your glasses from scratches and keep them clean in this cushioned pouch, which has a special frame to make it very easy to open and close. This project doesn't take very much fabric at all. It is a little fiddly to make, but results in an impressive gift.

Find the template on page 140

You will need
½ fat quarter of outer fabric
½ fat quarter of lining fabric
18 x 8½in (46 x 21.5cm) each of iron-on adhesive and wadding (or iron-on wadding)
4in (10cm) glasses case flex frame
Tracing paper or greaseproof paper
Pencil
Scissors
Tape measure or ruler
Small pliers or tweezers
Sewing machine
Thread to match fabric
Zipper foot (optional)
Sewing needle
Pins
Dress-making scissors
Knitting needle for pushing out corners
Pen or fabric marker
Iron

NOTE: One fat quarter of fabric will make one glasses pouch if you use the same material for the lining.

1 Use the template on page 140 to cut out the fabrics, wadding and iron-on adhesive. Take the two pieces of outer fabric and fuse the wadding to the wrong side of each using the iron-on adhesive and a hot iron.

2 Pin or tack the two pieces of outer fabric right sides together, aligning all the edges. Starting at the point marked 'A' on the template, sew a 3/8in (1cm) seam around three sides to the point marked 'B' on the template. Reverse stitch as you start and finish for extra strength (see page 18).

3 Repeat step 1 with the lining fabrics, but this time leave a turning gap as indicated with Xs on the template.

4 Take the outer piece, still wrong sides out, and cut into the seam allowance at a 45-degree angle at point A. Trim from point A down to the bottom edge, to about 3/16in (5mm) from the stitch line. Do the same down the other side, from point B to the bottom edge. Trim off the same amount along the bottom edge, clipping the two corners diagonally (see page 27).

5 Press open the side seams of the lining before turning it right side out and slotting it inside the outer piece, right sides facing.

6 Push the lining right down inside using your fingers or a blunt tool such as a knitting needle to make sure the lining is fitted snugly. Now take the top of the lining fabric on one side and match it up to the top of the corresponding outer fabric top right sides together. Align the raw edges and pin or tack around the two top 'flaps' from point A to point B on both sides.

7 Starting from point A, sew around to point B – lower your machine needle by turning the wheel before you start so that you can be accurate in your starting position. Do the same with the other flap before trimming around the seams as you did in step 4, but leaving the seam allowance 3/8in (1cm) wide at A and B. Clip the top corners diagonally.

8 Turn your work right sides out gently through the turning gap. Fold the raw edges in at the gap and close it neatly by hand with overstitch (see page 15).

9 Push the lining back down snugly inside the padded outer. Use a blunt tool such as a knitting needle to prod the bottom corners from the inside to make them nice and sharp. You can use a pin to pick out the four top corners to make them as neat as you can.

10 Create the channels for the flex frame. Fold the two top flaps half down into the case so that the top corners meet with points A and B. Pin or tack in place. Sew as close to the edge as you can from A to B on each side, reverse stitching as you start and finish. This is more easily done with a zipper foot.

11 Open the flex frame and push the end of each arm through the channels you created in step 10. Do this gently so that the open hinge doesn't snag on the fabric inside the channels.

12 At the other side, fit both halves of the hinge together and use small tweezers or pliers to slot the tiny metal pin back into the hinge. Bend down the cap end to hold the pin permanently in place.

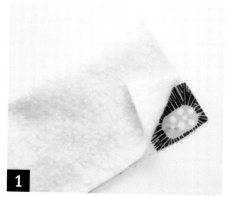

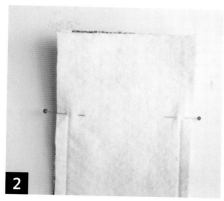

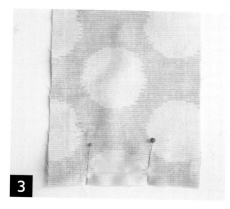

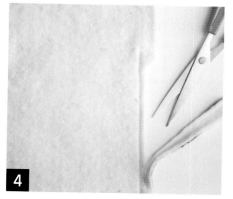

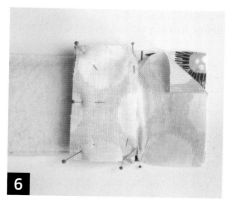

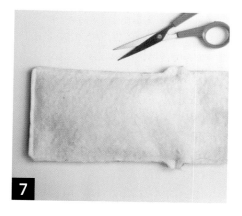

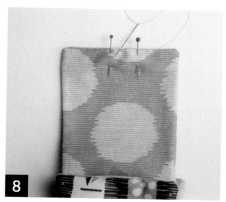

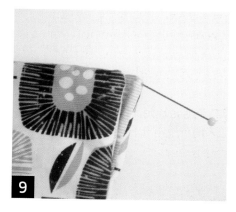

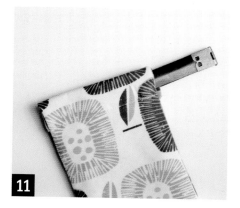

PAPERWEIGHT

This little paperweight is a quick make using just 10 x 5in (25 x 12.5cm) of fabric and a couple of handfuls of split peas! You can increase the amount of fabric and make a larger version for a doorstop, or smaller ones for tailor's pattern weights.

You will need
10 x 5in (25 x 12.5cm) outer fabric
10 x 3in (25 x 7.5cm) fusible heavyweight interfacing
2in (5cm) of ¾in (2cm)-wide herringbone tape
¾in (2cm) chrome 'D' ring
3½oz (100g) of split peas or lentils for filling
Tape measure or ruler
Sewing machine
Thread to match fabric
Sewing needle
Pins
Dress-making scissors
Pen or fabric marker
Iron
Knitting needle or other blunt tool for pushing out corners

NOTE: One fat quarter will make four paperweights.

1 Place the interfacing on the wrong side of the fabric and centre it so that you have 1in (2.5cm) overhang of fabric on either side: double-check that you've laid the interfacing glue side down. Fuse together with a hot iron. Top stitch $\frac{1}{16}$in (2mm) in from the two long edges of the interfacing to anchor it to the fabric (see page 16).

2 Take the piece of tape and feed it through the 'D' ring. Fold it over the flat side of the ring, aligning the raw edges, and machine stitch back and forth a couple of times to secure it in place.

3 Turn your work so that the right side of the fabric is facing you. Pin or tack the 'D' ring in position at the middle of the top short end and with the raw ends of the tape extending $\frac{3}{8}$in (5mm) beyond the edge of the fabric.

4 Fold up the bottom edge of your work to cover the 'D' ring and align the top raw edges. Pin or tack the side edges, marking a 2in (5cm) turning gap on the left-hand side starting 2in (5cm) from the bottom corner. Stitch $\frac{3}{8}$in (1cm) seams along both edges, leaving the turning gap open and reverse stitching at the beginning and end of each line of stitching – this is especially important at the gap to give it extra strength.

5 Press the two side seams open. This is fairly fiddly so be careful not to scorch your fingertips. Flatten the two bottom corners (see box corners, page 25) and stitch across them through the fabric only, just beyond the edge of the interfacing. There's no need to clip these box corners off.

6 Turn your work carefully through the turning gap. Prod the corners from the inside with a blunt tool such as a knitting needle, and pick at them from the outside to make them satisfyingly sharp. Press before spooning or pouring the split peas into it through the gap.

7 Turn the raw edge in at the turning gap and pin or tack it shut before closing it by hand using overstitch (see page 15).

8 Use your fingers to push the top two corners in – beneath the 'D' ring – so that they meet. Use doubled thread on a needle to hand stitch the two corners together – three or four stitches should be sufficient. Your stitches won't show, so don't worry too much about the neatness so much as their strength.

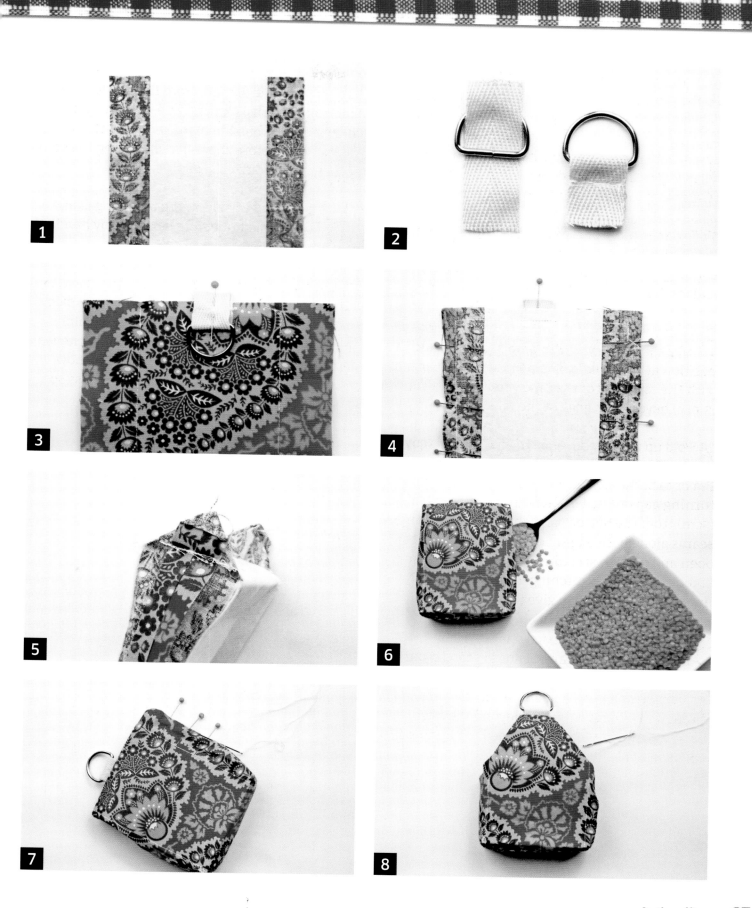

YO-YO CUSHION COVER

This pretty little cushion is perfect on an office chair, a bed or a sofa. Natural linen is beautifully simple yet luxurious, and the flower-like yo-yos create an attractive panel in the middle. This is a good project for using up interesting fabric scraps.

You will need
1 fat quarter of linen
15 scraps of fabric, each measuring at least 4½in (11.5cm) square
1¾in (4.5cm) yo-yo maker
14in (36cm) zip
18 x 12in (45 x 30cm) cushion pad
Sewing machine
Thread to match fabric
Sewing needle
Pins
Dress-making scissors
Pen or fabric marker
Iron
Knitting needle or other blunt tool for pushing out corners

1 Make 15 yo-yos following the instructions on page 23. Your panel will measure five yo-yos by three, so decide how to arrange them. Start sewing the yo-yos together, holding them face to face or right sides down. Sew about ³⁄₈in (1cm) of overstitch (see page 15) to join them together.

2 Stitch the top five yo-yos together in a row. Do the same with the two rows of five below. Now sew the rows of yo-yos together, each time sewing the edges together for ³⁄₈in (1cm) where their edges touch.

3 Zigzag stitch all around the raw edges of the piece of linen to reduce fraying. Fold over one short end of the fabric to lie 1in (2.5cm) below the other and press the fold with a hot iron. Fold it the other way, align the edges and press again where the new fold bisects the previous pressing. Open your fabric out. You now have creases that will help you to position the yo-yo panel on the cushion cover.

4 Position the yo-yo panel on the linen. Place the centre of the middle yo-yo at the point where the creases cross. This should leave about 5in (12.75cm) on either side between the yo-yo panel and the long raw edges of the linen. Pin down all the way around, then sew to the linen by hand using overstitch.

5 Fold your work in half, right sides facing, so that the two short ends of the linen align. Pin or tack along this edge and stitch ³⁄₈in (1cm) seams for just 2in (5cm) at either end of this edge. Press the seam open.

6 Place your zip right side down over the gap in the seam and tack it in place. Turn your work right side up and check that you're happy with the zip opening and the position of your tacking, which you will follow when stitching in the zip.

7 Using the zipper foot on your machine, stitch all the way around ³⁄₁₆in (5mm) from the zip teeth, following your tacking line and reversing back and forth at either short end for strength (see page 18). Turn your work inside out, and with the tube of linen right sides together, press it flat so that the zip lies 1in (2.5cm) from the bottom folded edge. Align and pin or tack the two raw sides – make sure that the zip is at least one-third open before you machine stitch ³⁄₈in (1cm) seams along each side.

8 Turn the cushion cover the right way out through the zip. Use the end of a knitting needle or other blunt tool to prod the corners from the inside. There's no need to clip these the corners; cushion pads rarely make their way right into the corners of a cushion cover, so the excess fabric helps to fill them. Finally, stuff the cover with your cushion pad and close the zip.

Tip

For a plump, well-filled cushion, your finished cover should be smaller than the cushion pad.

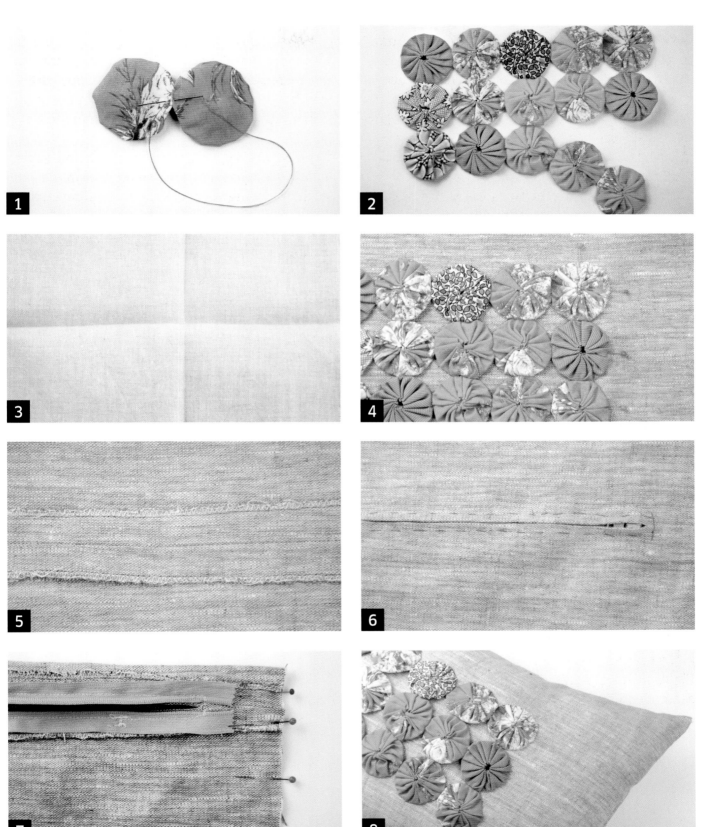

BEDROOM & BATHROOM

GUEST HAND TOWEL

Customize a plain towel with pretty pieces of fabric to make a guest feel special. You can use a solid piece of fabric with a contrasting hanging loop instead of fabric scraps and embellish it with trims and ribbons, or covered piping cord in place of the frill if you wish.

You will need
Scraps of fabric each measuring 1½ x 4in (4cm x 10cm)
   to make up a piece the size of your panel plus ³/8in (1cm)
   all the way around
Or: 1 fat quarter of fabric cut to the width of your towel and the
   depth of the towel's panel plus ³/8in (1cm) all the way around
   – in which case, leave out steps 1–5
Strip of fabric one and a half times the width of your towel
   by 1½in (4cm) for the ruffle (you may have to piece strips
   together to achieve the measurements required)
Scrap of fabric for the hanging loop
12in (30cm) string
Tape measure or ruler
Sewing machine
Thread to match fabric
Sewing needle
Pins
Dress-making scissors
Pen or fabric marker
Iron

NOTE: This guest towel measures 35½ x 19¾in (90 x 50cm).
Most towels have a solid panel, at least at one end – this is the
area covered here, and it measured 19¾ x 2¾in (50 x 7cm). If you
have no panel, simply follow the measurements given in step 8.

1 Make a hanging loop (see page 21). Cut the loop to measure 6in (15cm). Mark the centre of one end of the towel with a pin. Position the loop 3/8in (1cm) to either side of this pin, with 3/8in (1cm) of each end extending over the edge and on to your towel. Pin or tack the loop in place before stitching back and forth across both sides to secure it firmly. Use thread to match the colour of your towel, otherwise the stitching will show on the other side.

2 Cut 26 strips in assorted fabrics: each strip should measure 1½ x 4in (4 x 10cm). Lay out the strips in the order you want them pieced together. Take the first two strips, place them right sides together, and pin or tack along one long edge.

3 Machine stitch a 3/8in (1cm) seam along the edge and press open.

4 Keep adding the strips in order, each time placing the fabrics right sides together, aligning the long edges, and pinning or tacking before stitching a 3/8in (1cm) seam. Press all the seams open as you go.

5 Turn your work right side out and press. Measure and trim your work so that it measures 1in (2.5cm) larger in height and in length to your towel's top panel.

6 Make the ruffle. Take a strip of fabric one and a half times the width of your towel by 1½in (4cm) and fold in either short end. Press the whole strip in half along its length.

7 With your machine set at its longest stitch, sew a line 3/16in (5mm) in from the raw edges, and another one just 1/8in (3mm) from the first one, about 5/16in (8mm) from the raw edges. Secure the threads at one end of the strip by tying a knot or finishing them off by hand with a needle. At the other end, take one tail from each line of stitching on one side of the fabric, and slowly pull them to start gathering the frill. Once you have the width you require (the width of your towel) tie the tail ends in a knot snugly against the fabric surface to retain the correct length. Distribute the gathering evenly with your fingers.

8 Place the towel down in front of you with the hanging loop at the top. Lay your frill strip across the width, with the raw edge away from you. Align the centre of the frill along the bottom line of your panel area. In this case, the panel is 2¾in (7cm) deep and 5/8in (1.5cm) has been left at the top edge, so the bottom of the panel is 3¾in (8.5cm) below the top. Pin or tack it in place.

9 Now take your pieced panel and lay it right side down over the frill, aligning its top raw edge with the raw edge of the frill. Pin or tack in position. You should have material extending beyond your towel on either side.

10 Stitch a seam along the panel, sewing through all layers 3/8in (1cm) from the aligned raw edges and reverse stitching at either end (see page 18). Fold the panel upwards towards the top edge of the towel and give it a press.

11 Fold the raw edge in all the way around and pin or tack in place.

12 Topstitch (see page 16) all around the panel 1/8in (3mm) from the edge. Finally, give your work a good press with a hot iron.

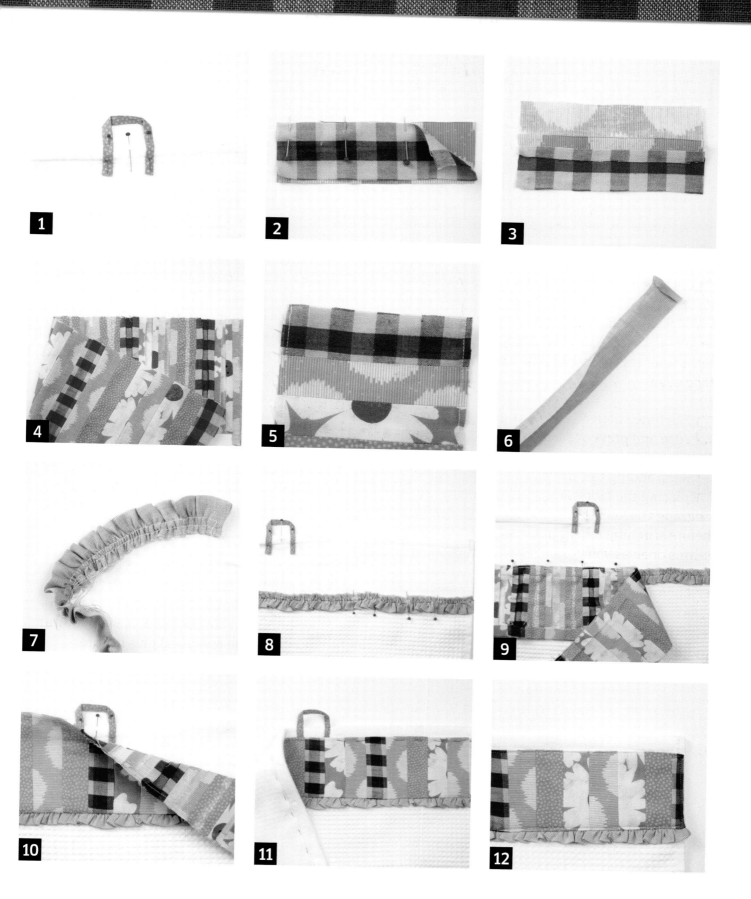

LAVENDER FLOWERS

Hang these sweet-smelling lavender flowers from your clothes hangers or tuck them among your linens. They will keep laundry fresh and help to repel moths. The flowers look cute on their own, or as a little bouquet of three or more.

Find the templates on page 143

You will need
8 x 4in (20 x 10cm) of floral fabric or 2 pieces 4in (10cm) square
Scrap of plain fabric at least 1½in (4cm) square
Scrap of fusible interfacing at least 1½in (4cm) square
³/8in (1cm) button
Roughly ½oz (15g) of dried lavender
120in (about 3m) of cotton embroidery thread
Tracing paper or baking parchment
Pencil
Scissors
Tape measure or ruler
Sewing machine
Thread to match fabric
Embroidery needle
Sewing needle
Pins
Dress-making scissors
Teaspoon
Pen or fabric marker
Paper or thin card
Iron

NOTE: One fat quarter will make five flowers.

1 Start by making your plain central petals. Fuse the piece of interfacing to the back of the plain fabric using a hot iron.

2 Using the template on page 143, cut out the petals.

3 Using the template, cut out two 4in (10cm) circles and place them right sides together.

4 Pin or tack the two circles together. Stitch a ³/8in (1cm) seam all around, leaving a 1¼in (3cm) turning gap as indicated by the Xs on the template. Reverse stitch at each side of the turning gap for extra strength (see page 18).

5 Cut little 'V's all around the seam allowance (see page 19l), apart from at the turning gap. Make sure you do not cut into the stitch line.

6 Turn your work right side out. Make a small funnel by using a piece of thin card or paper roughly 6 x 4in (15 x 10cm) and secure it with a pin. Slot the narrow end of the paper funnel into the turning gap and start filling your fabric with dried lavender. Use a teaspoon for this – the handle will come in useful if you need to prod or push in the lavender.

7 Do not over-stuff your bag – you need to have enough space for cinching the six segments later on. Fold in the raw edge at the turning gap and pin or tack together. Close it by hand with overstitch (see page 15).

8 Thread about 60in (1.5m) of embroidery thread on to the embroidery needle and pull the thread so that the ends meet and the thread is doubled – there's no need to tie a knot at the end. Place the plain flower centrally on the stuffed fabric. Hold the petals in position and insert the needle through the centre of the back of the lavender pad, through to the front and through the centre of the petals, ensuring you leave a 6in (15cm) tail at the back of your work.

9 Create the six flower segments by making large stitches to bind and cinch the edge of the pad. Each stitch should pass between two of the plain fabric petals and over the edge of the pad. Insert the needle through the centre of the back and out through the centre of the front again. Working the binding stitches between the petals will help you to divide the flower into fairly even sixths. With each large binding stitch, tug the thread firmly but not too tightly to create nice curved segments.

10 Continue stitching around until you have completed all six segments. You will get some puckering in the fabric, but this can be tweaked and smoothed at the end.

11 Leave your needle at the front of the work and use it to stitch on the button. With the needle at the back of your work, tie the remainder of the thread to the initial tail end in a tight knot. Push the needle up through the pad and out at the side seam in the middle of one segment edge. Create a button loop (see page 21).

12 Thread tail ends of thread through the embroidery needle and 'lose' them in the pad – to do this, push the needle through the pad at the centre of the back and out anywhere along the side seam. Trim the tail ends flush with the surface of the fabric.

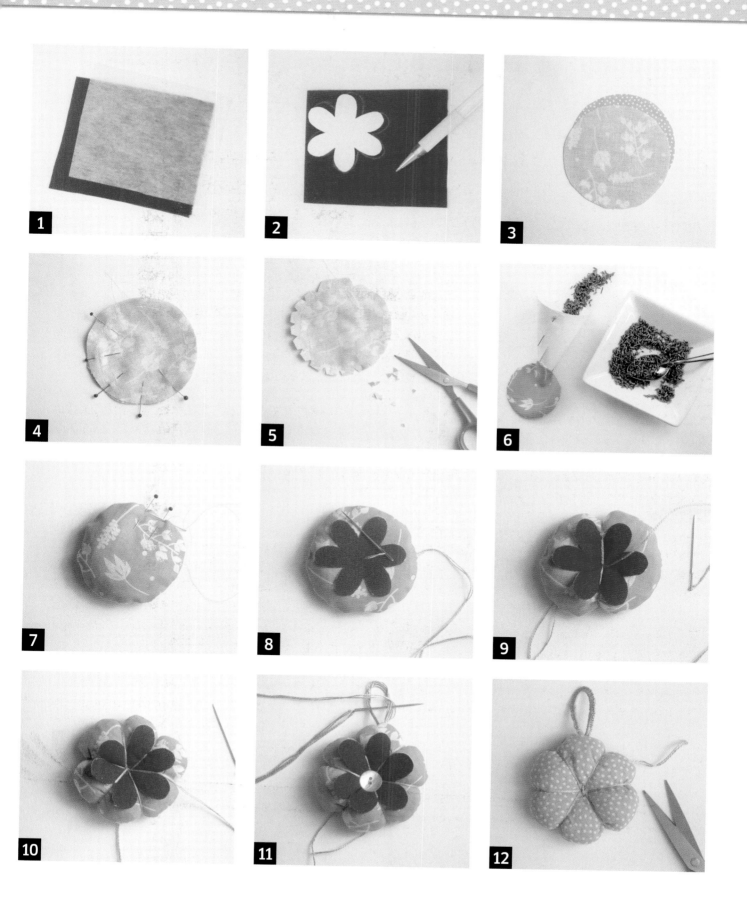

TISSUE HOLDER

Pretty and handy, this soft bag is perfect for storing paper tissues, and is so much more attractive than a plastic pouch. Rickrack is one of my favourite embellishments; it has a hint of vintage style, yet it is not overly fussy.

Find the template on page 139

You will need
9 x 6in (23 x 15cm) of outer fabric
9 x 6in (23 x 15cm) of plain lining fabric
15in (38cm) of rickrack
Tracing paper or baking parchment
Pencil
Scissors
Tape measure or ruler
Sewing machine and thread
Needle and thread
Pins
Dress-making scissors
Pen or fabric marker
Iron
Knitting needle and pin for pushing out corners

NOTE: One fat quarter will make three holders with the same outer and lining material.

1 Cut out the pieces of fabric using the template on page 139. With the lining fabric right side up, tack a piece of rickrack along the curved edge at one end. Take care to align the top of the rickrack with the raw edge of the lining fabric, and tack accurately along the centre of the trim. You will be using this tacking to guide your machine stitching. Repeat this along the other curved edge of the lining fabric.

2 Lay the piece of outer fabric face down on top of the lining so that the pieces lie right sides together. Pin or tack all the way around, aligning the raw edges carefully. If you tack, use a different colour thread to the one you used to secure your rickrack. Mark a turning gap between the Xs indicated on the template along one straight edge.

3 With the lining side facing you, start at one side of the turning gap, reverse stitching for extra strength, and stitch a straight ³/₈in (1cm) seam to the corner. Turn the corner, then sew slowly along the tack line from step 1 – the stitching should run directly through the centre of the rickrack. Continue until you reach the other side of the gap. Reverse stitch and finish (see page 18). Snip the corners.

4 Turn your work right side out. Prod the corners from the inside with the end of a knitting needle to make them sharp and pick at them from the outside with a pin.

Tip

When turning corners, remember to leave the needle in the fabric, raise the foot, pivot the fabric and lower the foot again to resume stitching.

5 Tuck the raw edge in at the turning gap and give the whole item a good press with a hot iron. Tack along the opening before sewing closed by hand with overstitch (see page 16).

6 With your work right side up facing you, the curved ends to the sides, fold in the sides so that the rickrack trim just meets in the middle. Manoeuvre the sides so that the right-hand point overlaps at the centre top and the left-hand side at the centre bottom. Press with a hot iron and pin or tack in place.

7 Stitch along each edge by machine through all the layers of fabric at the same time, as close to the edge as you can.

8 Turn your work right side out through the rickrack-trimmed opening. Use a knitting needle from the inside and a pin from the outside to make the four corners as sharp as possible. Give a final press with a hot iron.

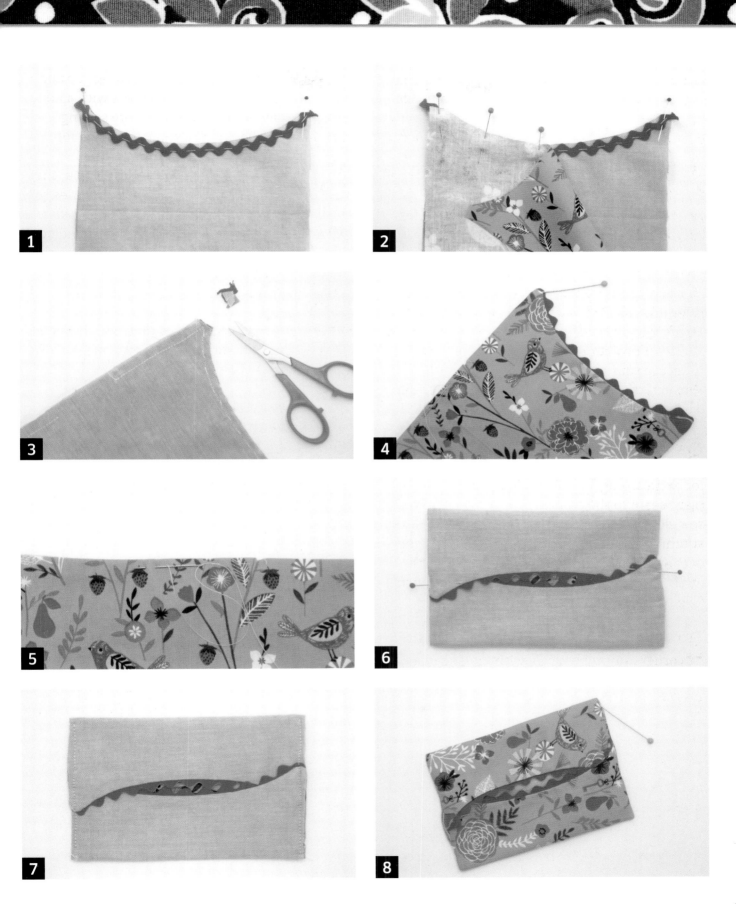

PADDED CLOTHES HANGER

Not simply nostalgic, this clothes hanger is also incredibly practical. The padding reduces creasing on your garments, while the pretty little frill stops finer, silkier and wide-necked items from slipping off. This is a lovely present to give along with a garment.

Find the template on page 138

You will need
1 wooden hanger – this one measures 17¾ x 1½in (45 x 4cm)
1 fat quarter of fabric for the cover
2 strips of 27½ x 1¼in (70 x 3cm) fabric for the frill – it can be made up from several pieces
2 pieces of 60 x 1½in (152 x 4cm) wadding
12in (30cm) length of ⅜in (1cm)-wide ribbon
Fabric glue (optional)
Tracing paper or baking parchment
Pen or pencil
Scissors
Tape measure or ruler
Sewing machine
Thread to match fabric
Sewing needle
Pins
Dress-making scissors
Pen or fabric marker
Iron
Knitting needle for pushing out corners

Tip
Use the small strips of wadding that are often left over from quilting projects to make these clothes hangers. That way, nothing goes to waste!

1 Take a strip of wadding. Starting just to one side of the hook of the hanger, wrap one strip of wadding once around the wood, catching the free end under your first wrap or anchoring it with a dab of fabric glue. Passing the wadding to the other side of the hook, continue wrapping the wadding around the wood. When you reach the end, use an 8in (20cm) piece of wadding folded over a few times to cover and cushion the end of the hanger. Hold it in place with a couple of dabs of fabric glue if you wish, before continuing wrapping the long strip over it.

2 Trim the end of the wadding strip. Pin it in place and hand stitch or glue the edge to anchor it. Repeat steps 1 and 2 to complete the wrapping of the other half of the hanger.

3 Make the frill. Taking one of the long fabric strips, fold in one short end to the wrong side, then fold the whole length in half, right sides together, to make a $^5/_8$in (1.5cm)-wide strip. Press with a hot iron.

4 Set your machine to its longest stitch. Start stitching $^3/_{16}$in (5mm) in from the raw edge of one end of the folded strip, and stitch to within $^3/_{16}$in (5mm) of the other end. This can also be done by hand with running stitch (see page 15) and your thread doubled. Pull one of the threads to gather the strip to fit the measurement around the template on page 138 from point A to point B.

5 Once you have gathered your frill to the required length, tie the threads in a firm knot at either end. Check the distribution of fabric across the strip before pressing it with a hot iron.

6 Cut four pieces of fabric using the template from page 138. Place one of these pieces face up in front of you and start to pin your frill around the edge, aligning its raw edges with the raw edge of the fabric piece. Work from point A all the way around to point B.

7 Now place another piece down on top of your prepared and pinned frill, right side down. Work your way around the edge, taking the pins that are anchoring the frill out and reusing them to pin through all the layers around the edge.

8 Stitch a $^3/_8$in (1cm) seam all the way around by machine, leaving the short straight end just beyond points A and B open. Work slowly around the curved end to achieve a nice, smooth stitch line. Turn your work right sides out through the open end using your fingers or a knitting needle.

9 Tweak and tease the frilled edge and press with a hot iron. Slip it onto one arm of your hanger. Do this slowly and carefully to avoid snagging and bunching the wadding. Tuck the raw edge in directly below the hook between points A and B on both sides of the hanger.

10 Repeat steps 4 to 10 to make the second half of the cover. Stitch the two halves together from point A to point B by hand on both sides using overstitch (see page 15).

11 Wrap the ribbon around the clothes hanger below the hook and tie a bow, positioning the ribbon so that it covers the central hand-stitched seams.

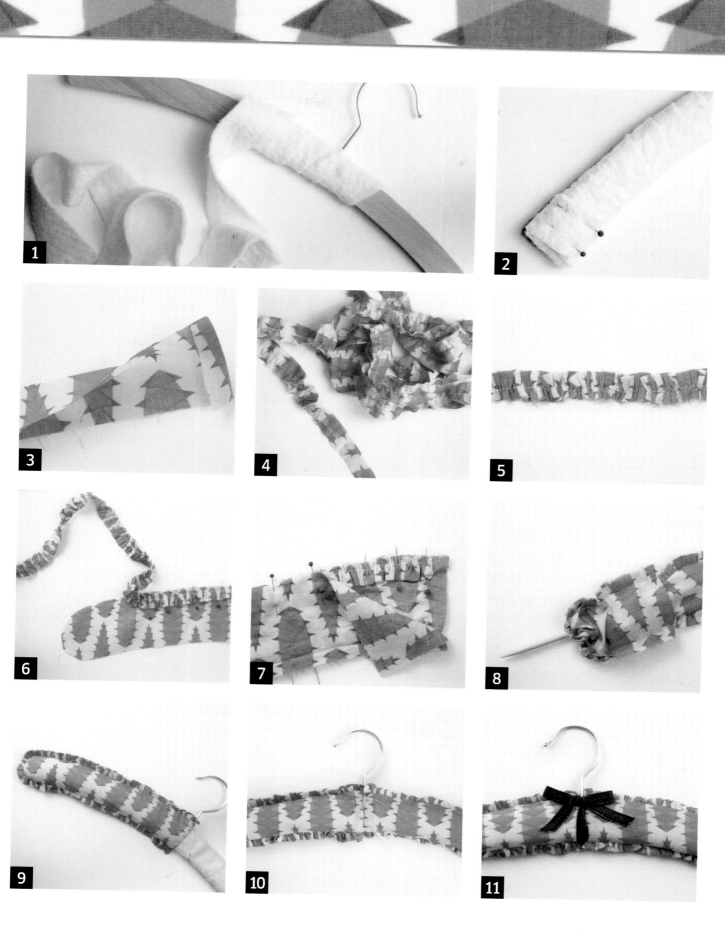

HAIRBRUSH BAG

Hung on a hook on the back of a door, this bag is great for keeping a hairbrush tidied away yet still within easy reach. It is also useful for holding keys and other small items. The bag can be made in any mixture of patterned or plain fabrics.

Find the templates on page 145

You will need
½ fat quarter of patterned outer fabric (for front)
½ fat quarter of plain outer fabric (for back)
1 fat quarter of lining fabric
22in (56cm) length of ¾in (2cm)-wide cotton herringbone tape
Tape measure or ruler
Tracing paper or baking parchment
Pencil
Scissors
Sewing machine
Thread to match fabric
Sewing needle
Pins
Pen or fabric marker
Dress-making scissors
Iron

NOTE: Two fat quarters (one outer, one lining), or four pieces of stash fabrics measuring 12 x 8½in (30 x 21.5cm), will make one bag.

1 Cut out the pieces using the templates on page 145. Lay lining piece A on top of one outer patterned piece A, right sides together. Align all the edges and pin or tack together around the teardrop edge.

2 Machine stitch a ³/₈in (1cm) seam around the inside edge of the work. Use sharp scissors to trim the seam allowance to ³/₁₆in (5mm) and turn right side out by pulling the patterned fabric through the teardrop.

3 Tease and tweak your stitched seam to make it as neat and sharp as possible before pressing with a hot iron.

4 Place your outer fabric piece B face down on top of your work, aligning the outside edges, and pin carefully all the way around. Take great care to pin it to the top layer of patterned fabric only.

5 Turn your work over so that the lining of the teardrop is facing you. Place your lining piece B face down on top of your work and align the outside edges of both lining pieces, right sides together. Pin the two layers together, again ensuring that you do not pick up either of the two outer layers as you do so.

6 Stitch ³/₈in (1cm) seams around the pinned edges of firstly the outer and then the lining fabric layers. Cut small 'V' shapes out of the seam allowance of the two bottom curves of both the outer and lining seams.

7 Press open the straight side seams of both the outer and lining fabrics. Turn the work through the gap in the top raw edges so that it finishes up with the lining pushed back inside the outer. Manipulate the edge of the teardrop so that it is crisp. Press with a hot iron.

8 Zigzag stitch along the top raw edges of the bag to hold all four layers in position.

9 Turn your work over so that the back is facing you. Find the centre of the herringbone tape and place it so that the centre of the top of the bag lines up with the centre of the tape and halfway across its width. Pin or tack your bag to the tape.

10 Fold down the tape to encase the top zigzagged edge of the bag. Pin or tack in place. Fold in each short end of the tape to prevent it fraying. Then sew just in from the edge, stitching from one end, across the top of the bag, to finish at the other end. Reverse stitch at either end for strength (see page 18).

11 Tie the two tape ends in a neat bow, ready to hang up the bag.

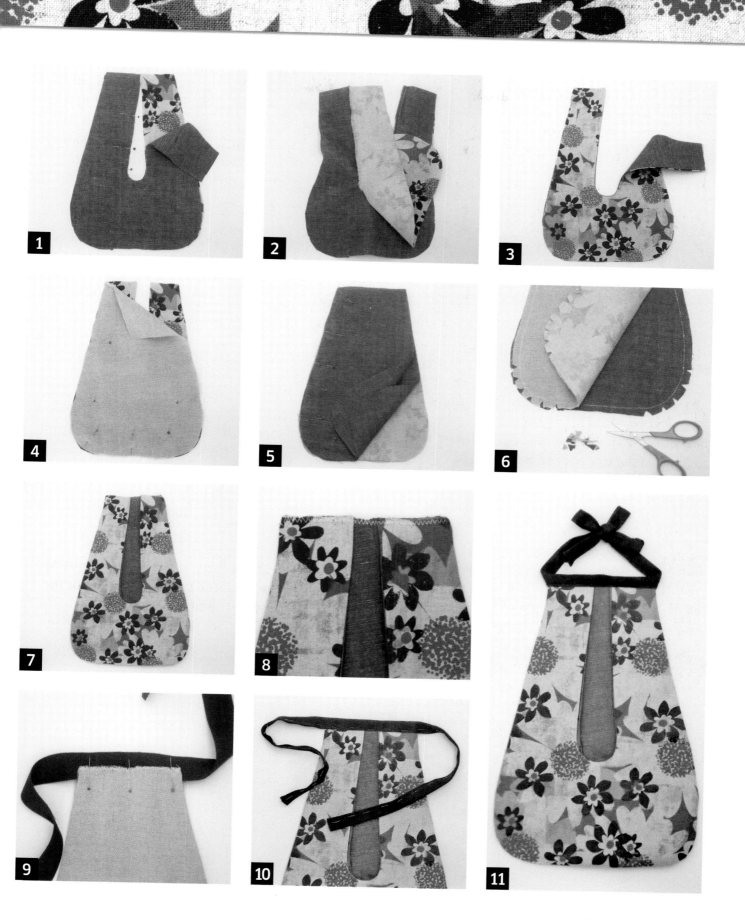

ACCESSORIES

DEEP PURSE

This purse can take on many guises as a gift: a sewing kit, make-up bag or a post-holiday foreign coin purse. You could scale it up to make it slightly bigger and attach a fine shoulder strap to make a neat sling purse.

Find the template on page 142

You will need
½ fat quarter of outer fabric
½ fat quarter of lining or contrasting fabric
4in (10cm) zip
Tracing paper or greaseproof paper
Pencil
Scissors
Tape measure or ruler
Pins
Sewing machine
Thread to match fabric
Zipper foot
Sewing needle
Dress-making scissors
Pen or fabric marker
Iron

NOTE: One fat quarter will make one purse with the same outer and lining fabric.

1 Use the template on page 142 to cut out the pieces. Make the two small pieces of lining or contrasting fabric, fold them in half and press with a hot iron. With the zip laid out right side up, tack one piece to the left-hand end of it, with the folded edge on the right. The fabric should overlap the end of the zip by ¾in (2cm). Tack the second piece to the right-hand end of the zip in the same way, its folded edge on the left. Trim the ends of both fabric scraps to lie flush with the ends of the zip.

2 Lay your outer fabric down in front of you right side up. Now lay the zip, wrong side up, on top of it along one short edge. Align the edge of the zip with the raw edge of the fabric and pin or tack in position. Now lay your lining fabric face down on top, aligning one of its short edges with the tacked-on zip. Pin or tack the lining fabric in position.

3 Stitch along the tacked or pinned line, using the zipper foot.

4 Fold the outer and lining fabrics away from the stitched seam and press with a hot iron. Place your work with the lining side facing you and your zip edge lying at the top. Fold up the bottom raw edge of the fabric to cover the zip and align with the top edge. Pin or tack in position. Turn your work over. You should have a loop of lining fabric at the back and the outer fabric on top in front of you.

5 Now fold up the bottom edge of the outer fabric – right sides facing – so that it covers the zip and aligns with the top edge of your work. Pin or tack in place. Stitch another seam (as you did in step 4) along this side of the zip through all layers. You now have two 'loops' of fabric attached to the zip.

6 Turn the work right sides out so that the 'loop' of lining lies within the 'loop' of outer fabric.

7 Lay the work out so that the zip is 1½in (4cm) from the top. Press with a hot iron. Make sure your zip is at least a third open and align the side seams before pinning or tacking along them.

8 Stitch a ³⁄₁₆in (5mm) seam down both sides. Snip off the corners diagonally (see page 19), taking care not to snip the stitching. Trim the seam allowance of both side seams down to ¹⁄₈in (3mm) with sharp scissors.

9 Turn your work inside out through the zip. Tweak the seams to make them sharp. Use a pin to pick carefully at the corners.

10 Give both side seams a really firm press with a hot iron and pin or tack along them. Stitch ³⁄₁₆in (5mm) seams along both sides. Press with the hot iron.

11 Flatten the two bottom corners and pin or tack. Press with a hot iron before marking a line ¾in (2cm) from the tip of each corner, using the box corner template. Stitch along these lines by machine.

12 Turn the work right side out through the zip and press the whole piece.

Tip

In step 3, use the outside edge of your machine's foot as a guide, lining it up with the fabric edge. Make sure that the stitch line is near to the zip teeth (about ¹⁄₈in/3mm), but not so close that it might interfere with the zip's function.

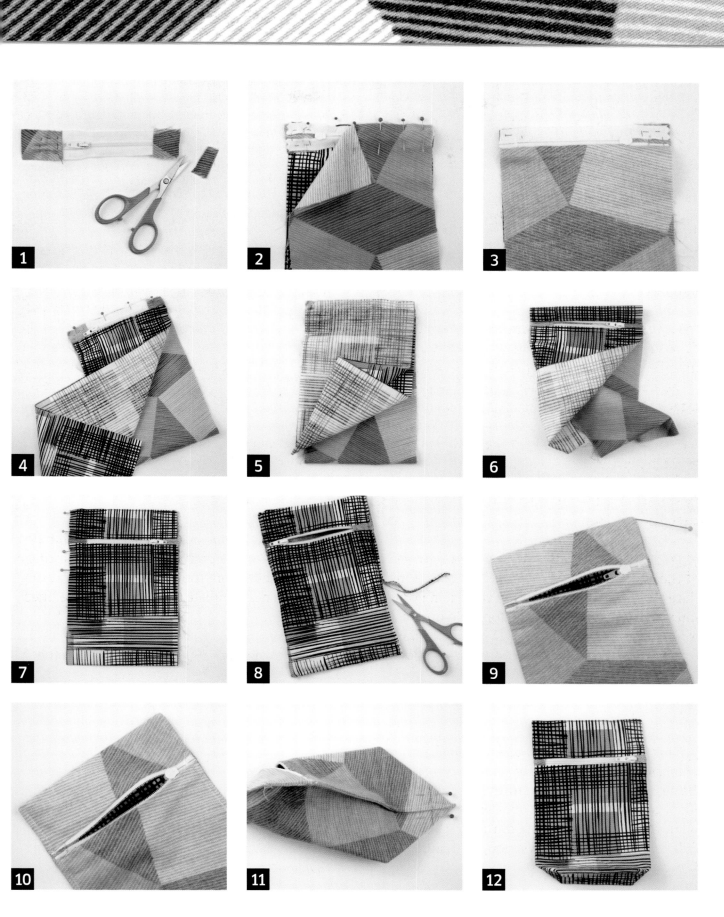

HAIR SCRUNCHIE

You can make one of these scrunchies in practically no time at all. Give one as an extra little gift, or make a selection from different scraps of fabric. Alternatively, you could join two strips of contrasting fabric to make a multi-coloured scrunchie.

You will need
16 x 4in (40.5 x 10cm) fabric
7in (18cm) of $^3/_8$in (1cm)-wide elastic
Tape measure or ruler
Sewing machine
Thread to match fabric
Sewing needle
Pins
Dress-making scissors
Pen or fabric marker
Iron
Safety pin

NOTE: One fat quarter will make five scrunchies.

1 Fold the fabric in half lengthways, right sides facing. Align all the raw edges and pin along the long edge. Sew a straight 3/8in (1cm) seam by machine along this edge. Start and finish 2in (5cm) in from either end and reverse stitch at these points for extra strength (see page 18).

2 Press open the seam before turning your work right side out. Place it in front of you horizontally with the seam side face down and then take the left-hand end and fold it over to meet the right-hand end. Align the two short ends and pin or tack them right sides together.

3 Stitch a 3/8in (1cm) seam along the short edge. Remove the pins or tacking. Press the new seam flat as well as you can before pushing it inside your work through the turning gap it has created. Tuck in the raw edges along this gap and give your work a press with a hot iron.

4 Attach a safety pin to one end of the length of elastic. Push this end in through the turning gap and around the tube of fabric to exit through the gap again.

5 Keeping a good hold of the two ends of the elastic, remove the safety pin and use a pin to hold the two ends together. Try to ensure that the elastic is not twisted, but it is not essential. Use a needle and thread to hand stitch the two ends firmly together.

6 Pin or tack the turning gap closed and then hand stitch along it using overstitch or hem stitch (see page 15).

Tip

This project particularly lends itself to customizing. Why not add a little lace or a pompom trim along the long seam?

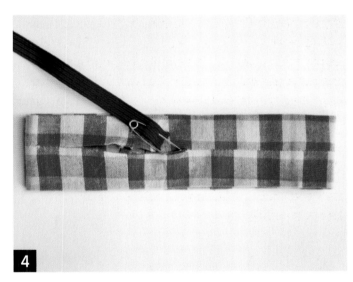

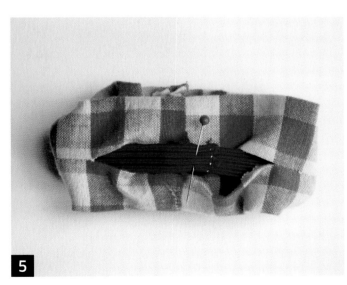

LINED SCARF

This lovely bespoke scarf can be made for any occasion by mixing and matching your patterns and fabrics. Make it with simple rickrack, coloured cotton lace or a simple tassel trim. The topstitching around the circumference gives an extra-special luxurious feel.

You will need
1 fat quarter of plain brushed cotton or fine wool fabric
1 fat quarter of patterned cotton
118in (3m) of tiny pompom trim
Tape measure or ruler
Sewing machine
Thread to match fabric
Zipper foot
Sewing needle
Pins
Dress-making scissors
Iron
Knitting needle for pushing out corners

NOTE: Cut each fat quarter in half and join together with a $3/8$in (1cm) seam (pressed open) to achieve the required measurements of 44 x 12$\frac{1}{2}$in (112 x 32cm) for each piece of fabric.

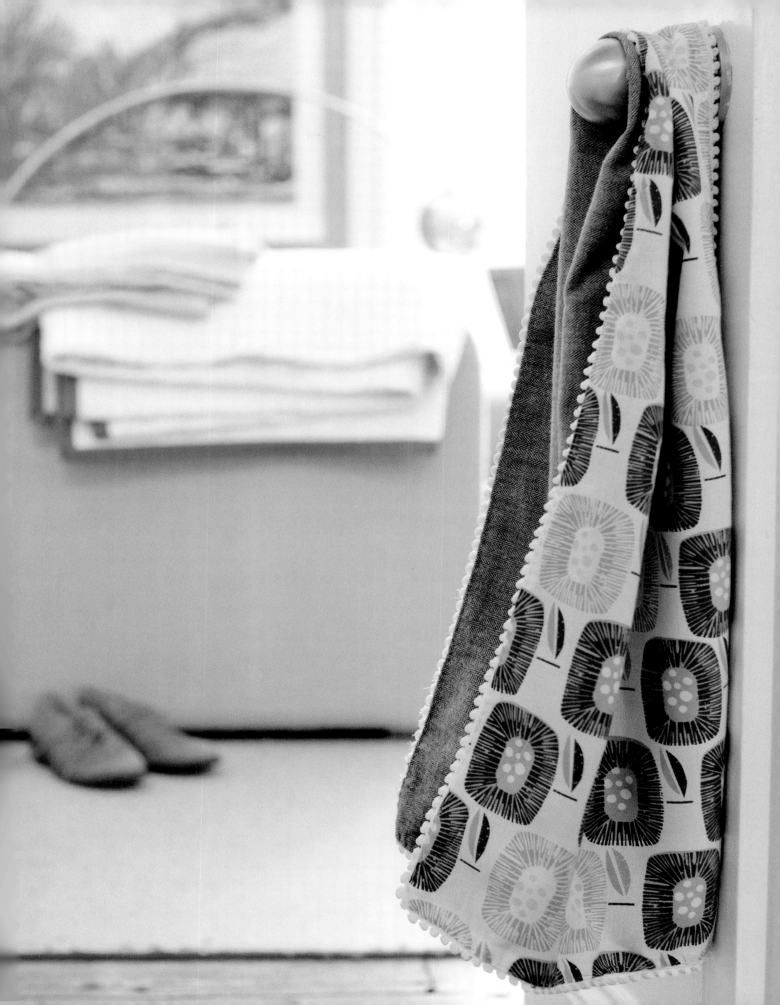

1 Take the brushed cotton or fine wool, and with the right side facing (if the fabric has one) start tacking the pompom trim all the way around. Turn ¾in (2cm) of the leading end over at 45 degrees. Position the trim carefully so that a ⅜in (1cm) seam will run just above the pompoms once stitched.

2 At the corner, ease the trim around the right angle so that it is very slightly curved – a soft curve works well here. When you have completed the circumference, turn the end of the trim up at 45 degrees to mirror the leading end, and trim to about ¾in (2cm).

3 With the patterned fabric face up, place the plain fabric right side down on top. Align all the edges and pin or tack together. If you tack, use a different colour thread to the one anchoring the trim. With the plain fabric facing you, and following the tacking anchoring the trim, stitch a ⅜in (1cm) seam all the way around your work, leaving a 4in (10cm) turning gap along one long edge. Reverse stitch at either side of the turning gap for strength (see page 18).

4 Trim the four corners of your work at 45 degrees to reduce bulk (see page 19). Turn it right sides out through the turning gap.

Tip
When sewing around the corners, go very slowly, raising the foot every couple of stitches with the needle down and pivoting your work before lowering the foot and stitching on.

5 Prod the corners of your scarf gently from inside through the turning gap with the end of a knitting needle. Tease and manipulate the seam all the way around to make the edges crisp. Press with a hot iron. Fold in the seam allowance along the closing gap and close it neatly by hand using overstitch (see page 15).

6 Press your work carefully again before stitching by hand through all layers evenly about ³/₁₆in (5mm) in from the trimmed edge using running stitch. You could do this on your sewing machine using topstitch (see page 16) if you prefer.

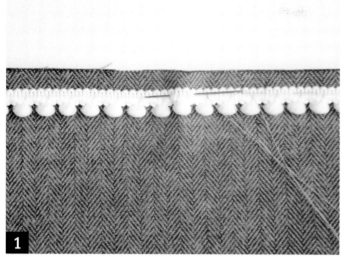

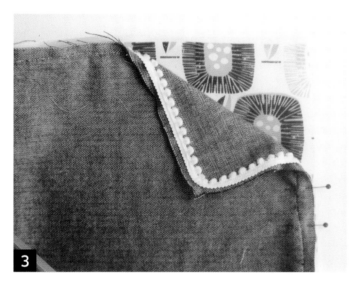

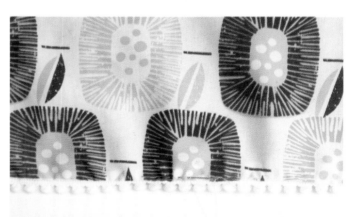

KEY FOB

A jolly bright key fob makes fishing for your keys easier and is a fabulously quick make. The fabric you choose helps you to personalize this gift for some lucky person. You could make a different one for each family member to avoid key confusions.

You will need
9 x 2in (23 x 5cm) patterned fabric
9 x 1in (23 x 2.5cm) heavy fabric stiffener
Two 9 x 1in (23 x 2.5cm) strips of iron-on adhesive
9in (23cm) length of 1in (2.5cm)-wide cotton tape
A scrap of fabric or wadding (see step 7)
Pair of pliers
1 metal key fob hardware set
Fabric glue
Sewing machine and thread
Sharp scissors
Iron

NOTE: This project is ideal for using up scraps from your stash. One fat quarter will make ten fobs from the same fabric.

1 Lay the patterned fabric right side down and fix one of the iron-on adhesive strips to it, positioning it centrally along its length, therefore leaving ½in (1.25cm) of fabric along either side. Take care to double-check that you have laid the strip glue side down before you use your iron. Lay the strip of stiffener down and use a hot iron to fuse the other adhesive strip to one side of it.

2 Peel the backing paper off the adhesive strip on the patterned fabric. Lay the strip of stiffener on top of the adhesive area, ensuring that you lay it plain side down – with its adhesive side upwards. Use a hot iron to fuse the stiffener to the fabric. Turn your work over and press again from the fabric side to ensure complete adhesion.

3 Turn your work back over again, wrong side facing you. Peel the backing paper off the strip of stiffener. Working carefully with the very tip of your iron, fold the edges of the fabric over as snugly as you can and adhere them to the stiffener. Be very careful not to get the adhesive on to your iron.

4 Now take your length of tape and lay it along your work so that it covers the raw edges of the patterned fabric. Align the edges carefully and use your iron to fix it along its centre where the adhesive is exposed between the edges of the fabric. This will hold it in place while you stitch in the next step.

5 Topstitch by machine ⅛in (3mm) in from both raw edges through all layers to give your fob crisp edges (see page 16).

6 Trim the ends of your work to make them nice and neat before fixing them into your key fob hardware. Run a small amount of fabric glue along the inside of the key fob hinge. Fold the fabric strip in half, tape sides together, and align the short edges. Tuck the ends firmly into the hinge of the key fob hardware.

7 Use a pair of pliers to close the hinge over the fabric. Cushion the mouth of the pliers with a scrap of fabric or wadding to avoid scratching the metal. Start pinching the hinge together in the middle, working out to either side. Squeeze as tightly as you can, bearing in mind that you don't want to crush the hinge.

8 Leave your work to one side for the fabric glue to set before adding the key ring.

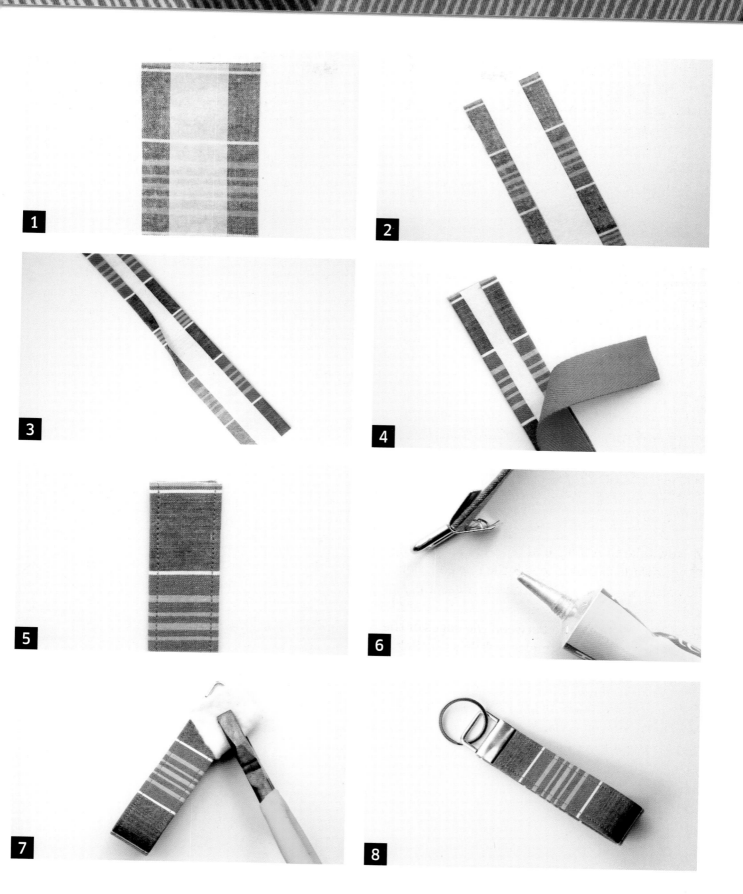

EARPHONE WALLET

This is a really simple design for a wallet to stop your earphones getting tangled up when you're not using them. You could also make it out of thick felt or leather, or embroider initials on it to make a more personalized present.

Find the template on page 138

You will need
2 pieces of fabric 4³/₈in (11cm) square
1 piece of heavy stabilizer 4³/₈in (11cm) square
16in (40.5cm) of 1in (2.5cm)-wide bias binding
12mm snap fastener kit
Hammer
Sewing machine
Thread to match fabric
Sewing needle
Pins
Dress-making scissors
Pen or fabric marker
Iron

NOTE: This project is ideal for using up scraps from your stash. If you use the same fabric for the outer and lining, one fat quarter will make five earphone wallets.

1 Use the template on page 138 to cut out the fabric pieces and stabilizer. Lay one piece of fabric (the lining) right side down, and then place the stabilizer on top. Place the second piece of fabric (the outer) right side up on top of the stabilizer.

2 Align all the raw edges so that you have the stabilizer sandwiched between the two fabrics, both of which have their right sides facing out. Use a hot iron to fuse all three layers together – this is most efficiently done if you iron on both sides. Machine stitch in large zigzags around the circumference through all three layers to prevent fraying while you work.

3 With the outer fabric facing you, open out the bias binding and place it right side down on the circle of fabric. Fold one end of the binding over by 3/16in (5mm) and position it so that the top/outer edge of it aligns with the raw edge of the fabric. Tack the binding to the circle of fabric all the way around, easing it carefully to fit, and align with the curved edge to make it as smooth a circle as you can. Tack along the fold crease in the bias binding near the edge of the circle. When you have completed the circumference, trim the bias binding so that it overlaps the other folded end by about 3/8in (1cm).

4 Machine sew around the bias binding. The stitch line should be along the binding fold where you have tacked it down. Work slowly in order to retain a smooth, even stitch line. Turn your work over. Fold the binding over the raw edge of the fabrics and pin it down, an inch (2.5cm) or so at a time. Sew down the binding by hand with hem stitch (see page 15).

5 Give both sides of your work a good press with a hot iron.

6 With your work right side up, mark a point 3/4in (2cm) from the edge, and another directly opposite it and 3/4in (2cm) from the edge. These points are for the snap fastener positioning. Follow the kit instructions to fix the two parts of a snap fastener in the positions you have just marked.

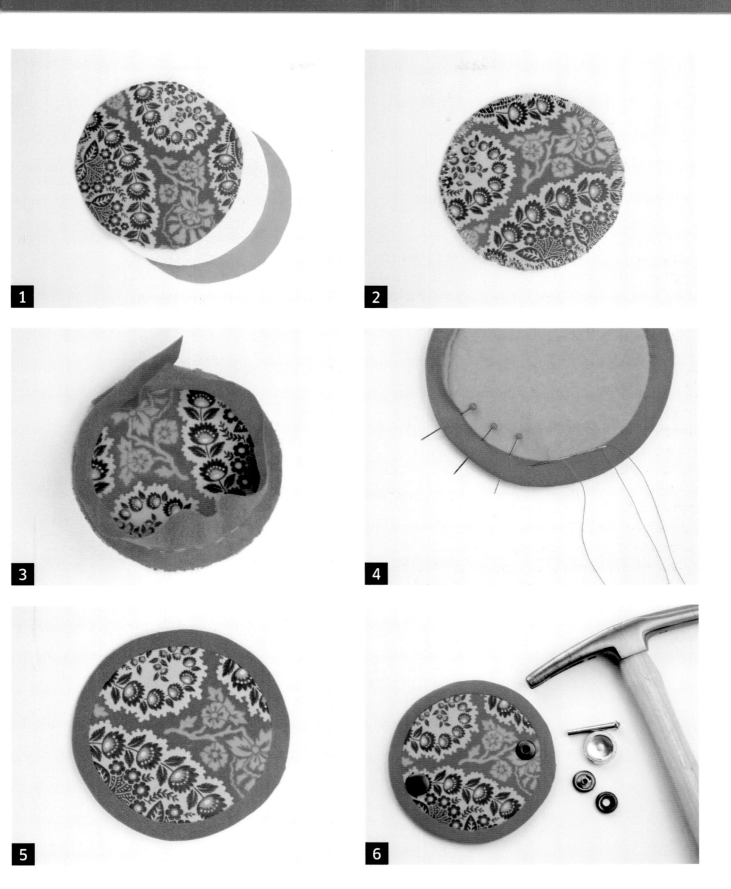

BAGS &
STORAGE

JEWELLERY POUCH

This is a great pouch for storing small items of jewellery. The internal pockets keep rings and pairs of earrings together to avoid tangles and scratches. You could resize the templates to make a bigger pouch to accommodate necklaces and bracelets.

Find the templates on page 148

You will need
2 fat quarters of outer fabric: you will need 2 circles 12in (30cm) in diameter
½ fat quarter of contrast fabric for the pockets: you will need 2 circles 7in (18cm) in diameter
1 circle of heavy fusible stabilizer 3⅛in (8cm) in diameter
60in (152cm) cotton or silk cord
2 small pieces of fusible interfacing, each 1½ x 1¼in (4 x 3cm)
Tracing paper or greaseproof paper
Pencil
Scissors
Tape measure or ruler
Safety pin
Sewing machine
Thread to match fabric
Sewing needle
Pins
Dress-making scissors
Pen or fabric marker
Iron

NOTE: You can make the whole pouch from two fat quarters if you use the same material for the pocket circles.

Tip
When sewing around the circles, stitch very slowly to achieve a smooth curve. If your machine has a speed restriction, use it.

1 Use the templates on page 148 to cut out the fabrics. Place the two smaller circles of fabric right sides together. Align the edges and pin or tack together. Slowly stitch a $^3/_8$in (1cm) seam all the way around, leaving a 2$^1/_2$in (5cm) gap as indicated on the template. Reverse stitch at either side of the gap for reinforcement (see page 18). Snip small 'V's around the seam allowance, except for the turning gap.

2 Turn your work right side out through the turning gap and fold in the raw edges. Press with a hot iron and close the turning gap by hand with overstitch (see page 15).

3 Take one of the large circles of outer fabric and fuse a piece of interfacing $^3/_4$in (2cm) below the centre of the top edge on the wrong side. Do the same at the bottom edge directly opposite the first one.

4 Make a buttonhole (see page 20) centred on each of the pieces of interfacing – they should lie perpendicular to the edge of the circle of fabric. Leave a 1$^1/_4$in (3cm) gap between the buttonholes and the curved raw fabric edge.

5 Place the two circles of outer fabric right sides together and pin or tack all the way around. Stitch a $^3/_8$in (1cm) seam, leaving a 2$^1/_2$in (5cm) turning gap, reverse stitching at either side. Trim the seam allowance to $^3/_{16}$in (5mm), apart from at the turning gap. There is no need to cut 'V's on this larger disc.

6 Turn your work right side out through the turning gap. Tweak the seam to make it as sharp as possible. Fold in the seam allowance on both sides of the turning gap. Press and close the opening by hand with overstitch.

7 Press again and make two complete circles of straight stitch by machine $^3/_4$in (2cm) and again 1$^1/_2$in (4cm) from the edge. The first of these should pass over the top of each of your buttonholes, the second through the bottom. You can draw guidelines for these circles with a fabric pen using paper templates 9$^1/_2$in and 8in (24cm and 20cm) in diameter. Stitch slowly to achieve neat circles.

8 Pin or tack the stabilizer to the centre of your pocket disc from step 3. Stitch the stabilizer to the fabric $^3/_{16}$in (5mm) from the edge.

9 Place the outer disc down so the side without the buttonholes is facing you. Centre the pocket disc on top, stabilizer side down. Pin or tack it in place. Stitch a circle just outside the stabilizer's edge – this will be $^3/_8$in (1cm) outside the stitched line from step 8.

10 Mark points around the outer edge of your pocket disc, dividing it into eight sections. Stitch from the circle of stitching from step 9 to the edge of the pocket disc to create eight separate pockets. Reverse stitch at the outer edge for strength (see page 18).

11 Turn your work over and use a needle to finish off the thread ends.

12 Cut the cord into two equal lengths. Use a safety pin to thread one piece through the cord channel, starting at one buttonhole, passing the opposite buttonhole and coming out again through the first buttonhole where it entered. Do the same with the second length of cord, this time starting and finishing through the other buttonhole. Finally, tie a tight knot to secure both ends of each cord.

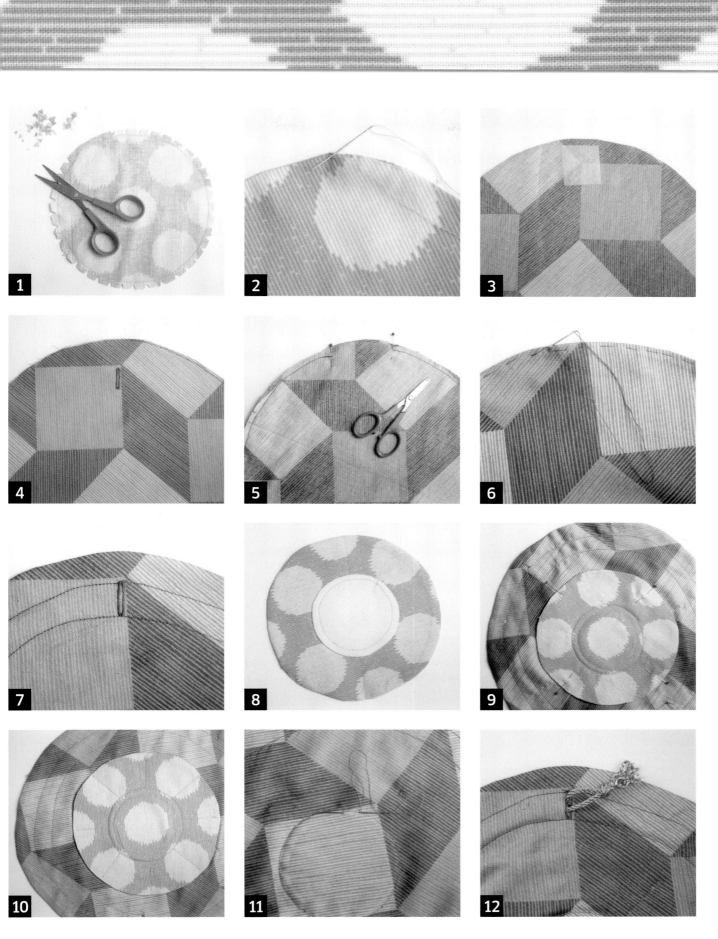

DRAWSTRING BAG

You can make this beautiful lined bag in any size. Bear in mind that if you make a small one, the top of the bag needs to fit over the sewing machine bed – on most machines you can remove a section of the bed to make it smaller.

Find the template on page 149

You will need
1 fat quarter of outer fabric
1½ fat quarters of lining fabric, to include four pieces measuring 4in (10cm) square for yo-yos and two strips of fabric 28 x 1¼in (71 x 3cm) pieced together for drawstrings, if making them
52in (132cm) cord or two strips of fabric 28 x 1¼in (71 x 3cm) fabric and 36in (91cm) string
Safety pin
Tape measure or ruler
Tracing paper or greaseproof paper
Pencil
Scissors
1¾in (4.5cm) yo-yo maker (optional)
Sewing machine
Thread to match fabric
Zipper foot
Sewing needle
Pins
Dress-making scissors
Knitting needle and pin for pushing out corners
Pen or fabric marker
Iron

1 Use the template on page 149 to cut out the fabrics. Take one piece of outer and one of lining fabric and place right sides together, aligning and pinning along one short edge.

2 Sew a ³∕8in (1cm) seam along this edge and press open with a hot iron. Do the same with the other pair of rectangular pieces. Place both pieces right sides together – the lining fabric ends together and the same with the outer fabrics. Pin all the way around, aligning the two central seams on each side.

3 Mark a turning gap with pins along one side of the lining as indicated on the template.

4 Mark two ³∕4in (2cm) gaps on the two outer fabric seams, 2in (5cm) below the centre seams. These will be the openings for the drawstring channels.

5 Sew a ³∕8in (1cm) seam all the way around, apart from the turning gap and the drawstring openings. Reverse stitch each time you start and stop stitching (see page 18). Trim the corners (see page 19). Press the side seams open.

6 Turn your work right sides out through the gap. Fold in the seam allowance on both sides of the gap. Pin or tack together before closing it by hand with overstitch (see page 15).

7 Push the lining down inside the outer fabric. Use a knitting needle to prod the bottom two corners from the inside, and a pin on the outside to make them sharp.

8 Tweak the seam around the top edge to make it neat. Press with a hot iron and then pin or tack around it. Topstitch all around the top by machine, ¹∕8in (3mm) from the edge (see page 16).

9 Mark the two drawstring openings with pins, 2in (5cm) from the top edge and ³∕4in (2cm) long. Pin or tack all around the bag in line with the top of the marked openings, 2in (5cm) from the top edge and through both layers of fabric. Work from the outside, and with your bag mouth fed over the bed of your machine to avoid accidentally stitching through all layers. Sew two parallel lines ³∕4in (2cm) apart, the first aligned with the top of the two outside openings and the second with the bottom of them – they should be 2in and 2³∕4in (5cm and 7cm) from the top edge.

10 If using cord, go to step 11. Otherwise, make your drawstrings (see page 22).

11 Use a safety pin to feed one drawstring or cord through the stitched channel on your bag. Enter through a drawstring gap on one side, around the circumference, and exit from the same gap you entered through.

12 Repeat step 11 with a second drawstring, this time entering and exiting from the opposite gap. Make four yo-yos using your yo-yo maker (see page 23). Place two drawstring ends so that they lie on the flat side of one yo-yo and sew to the centre of the yo-yo by hand using overstitch. Then stitch two yo-yos together, sandwiching the ends of the drawstrings between them. Sew all around their edges by hand using overstitch. Repeat this process with the other drawstring.

Tip

In step 8, so that your topstitch matches the fabrics, stitch with the outside of the bag facing you, with thread to match the outer fabric on the machine and thread to match the lining on the bobbin.

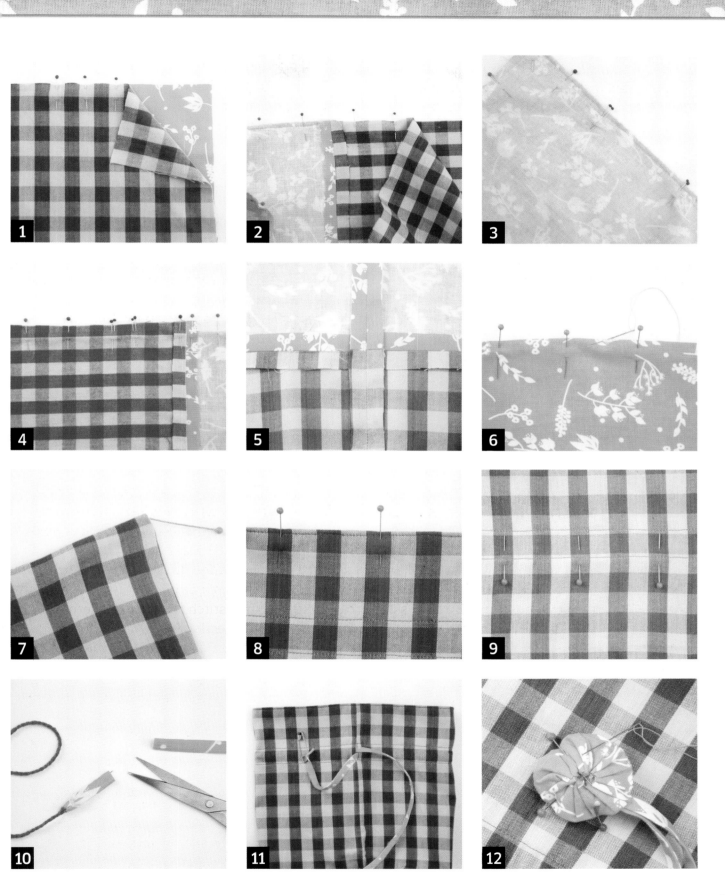

FABRIC ENVELOPE

This pretty fabric envelope has a hand-stitched button loop to secure the contents, and makes the perfect luxury packaging for jewellery, a gift voucher or a handkerchief. The project requires just two small pieces of fabric, a button and some embroidery cotton.

Find the template on page 144

You will need
10in (25cm) square outer fabric
10in (25cm) square lining fabric
Embroidery cotton or crochet cotton
1 x ½in (1.25cm) button
Tracing paper or greaseproof paper
Pencil
Scissors
Tape measure or ruler
Sewing machine
Thread to match fabric
Dress-making scissors
Pins
Sewing needle
Embroidery needle
Iron
Pen or fabric marker
Knitting needle for pushing out corners

NOTE: One fat quarter will make two envelopes with the same outer and lining fabric.

1 Use the template on page 144 to cut out the outer fabric and lining pieces. Take the outer fabric and fold it, right sides together, so that point A meets point AA. Pin or tack along these two seams, ensuring that the raw edges align. Stitch a 3/8in (1cm) seam along this edge.

2 Fold your fabric, right sides together, so that point B meets point BB. Pin or tack along this edge as before. Stitch a 3/8in (1cm) seam along this edge.

3 Press both seams open with a hot iron, taking care not to burn your fingers.

4 Repeat steps 1 and 2 with the lining fabric, but this time remember to leave a turning gap of 1 3/4in (4.5cm) on one seam between the two points marked 'X' on the template.

5 Press the seams of the lining open with a hot iron. Turn the outer piece right sides out and slot it into the lining piece, which is still wrong sides out.

6 Pushing your outer piece snugly within the lining, align all the raw edges around the opening and tack them together neatly.

7 Sew a 3/8in (1 cm) seam all around the top edge and remove the tacking stitches.

8 Turn the envelope right sides out through the turning gap in the lining.

9 Close the gap by hand with overstitch (see page 15) or hem stitch (see page 15).

10 Push the lining down into the outer fabric, using your fingers or the end of a knitting needle, to make sure the corners of the lining fit snugly into the corners of the outer fabric. Tease and tweak the seam around the opening of your fabric envelope to make it sharp. Give it a good press with a hot iron to make a crisp edge.

11 Thread an embroidery needle with doubled embroidery cotton or crochet cotton. Make a button loop large enough to fit over your button (see page 21).

12 Sew on the button (see page 21) to fit through the button loop.

Tip

In step 11, slip your initial loops over your button before you start the blanket stitching to check that the button fits through it easily and is not too tight.

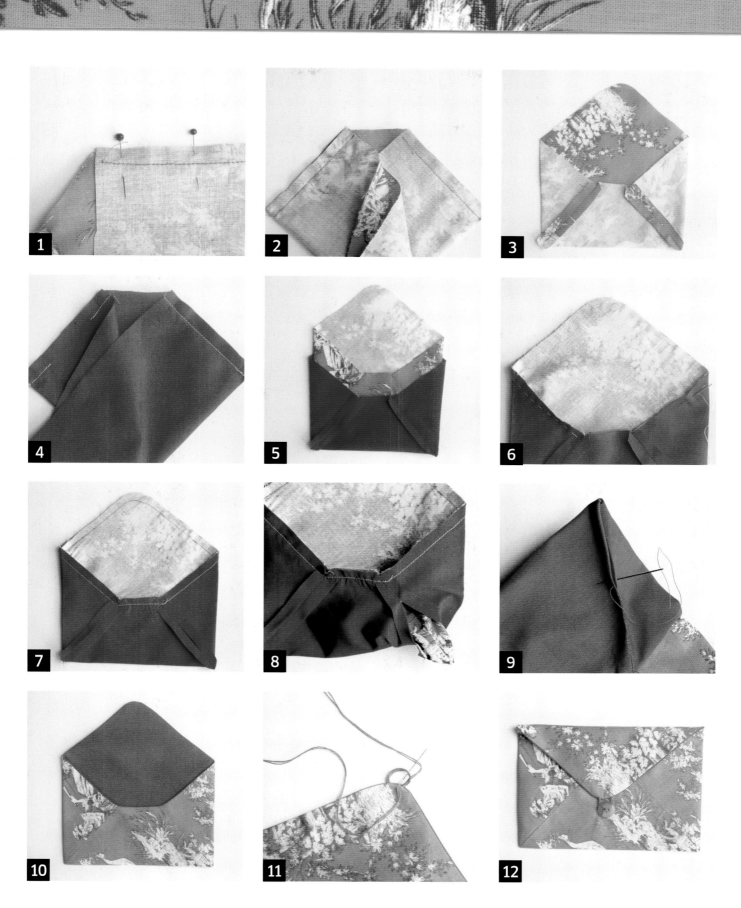

CARD WALLET

This is a great little fabric card wallet to help keep life in order. The project uses quite small amounts of fabric and could be made out of many combinations of colours and patterns from your stash, as long as your fabric is not too thick.

Find the templates on page 146

You will need
$6^5/8$ x $4^1/2$in (17 x 11.5cm) of outer fabric
1 fat quarter of contrast fabric
$15^1/2$ x 14in (39 x 35cm) fusible interfacing
6 x $3^3/4$in (15 x 9.5cm) fusible heavyweight stabilizer
6in (15cm) of $^3/8$in (1cm)-wide elastic
Tracing paper or greaseproof paper
Pencil
Scissors
Sewing machine and thread
Needle and thread
Pins
Tape measure or ruler
Dress-making scissors
Pen or fabric marker
Iron
Knitting needle or other blunt tool for pushing out corners

NOTE: One fat quarter will make two wallets in the same outer and lining fabric, or you can use stash fabrics for each piece.

1 Use the templates on page 146 to cut out the outer fabric, lining, interfacing and stabilizer. With the iron, fuse the stabilizer to the centre of the wrong side of your outer piece, leaving a ³⁄₈in (1cm) seam allowance all the way around. Fuse the interfacing to the centre of the wrong side of each of the four pocket pieces, again leaving a ³⁄₈in (1cm) seam allowance all the way around.

2 Turn your outer fabric right side up and lay it horizontally in front of you. Lay the piece of elastic vertically 1in (2.5cm) from the right-hand edge. Use your machine to reverse stitch back and forth several times ³⁄₈in (1cm) from the top and bottom (see page 18). Take note that your stitching will be through the outer fabric only, close to the edge but not through the stabilizer.

3 Fold one of the short pocket pieces in half, wrong sides together as indicated on the template, and press with an iron. Topstitch along the fold, ¹⁄₈in (3mm) from the edge (see page 16). Repeat with the three remaining pocket pieces.

4 Lay the lining piece down in front of you right side up. Place one tall pocket piece on top of it so that the raw edges along one edge of it align with the raw edges of the left-hand side of the lining piece. Pin or tack along this edge. Do the same with the tall pocket on the other side.

5 Stitch a ³⁄₄in (2cm) seam along both side edges. Trim the seam allowances down to ³⁄₁₆in (5mm).

6 Place a short pocket piece over one of the tall pocket pieces so that its topstitched edge lies 1in (2.5cm) below the top edge of the tall pocket and its long raw edge lies beyond the trimmed seam of the tall pocket behind it (from step 5). Pin the small pocket in position. Topstitch ³⁄₁₆in

(5mm) from the raw top and bottom edges to hold the short pocket in position. Repeat with the other short pocket piece on the other side.

7 Place the lining and pocket pieces right sides together on top of the outer piece, aligning all the raw edges. The lining piece will be ³⁄₄in (2cm) shorter than the short pocket and outer pieces at the bottom edge. Pin or tack in position. Sew a ³⁄₈in (1cm) seam along both the top and the bottom edges, reverse stitching at the beginning and end for strength. Trim the seams down to ³⁄₁₆in (5mm). Clip the two top corners diagonally.

8 Slip your hand through one of the open side edges, in between the tall and short pocket layers, and turn the work out gently through this gap. You will end up with the tall pockets on the lining side of your work.

9 The short pockets will be on the outer side of your work. The wallet may look a bit wonky, and the pockets will slightly distort the stabilizer shape, but this will be reduced at the next stage. Pin or tack along the two raw side edges.

10 Stitch a ³⁄₈in (1cm) hem along both raw edges, reversing at each end. Clip the corners again if necessary. Turn the short pockets over to the lining side, encasing the raw seam allowance inside the small pockets.

11 Prod the corners from inside the pockets with a blunt tool such as a knitting needle, and use a pin to pick at the four corners to make them nice and sharp.

12 Press your work with a hot iron – don't let the iron linger too long over the elastic.

SHOPPING BAG

This capacious bag has handles wrapped all the way to the bottom for strength, and a convenient outside pocket, so there'll be no need to rummage to the bottom of the bag for keys when reaching the front door.

You will need

2 fat quarters of patterned fabric: 2 pieces 18 x 12½in (45.5 x 32cm) for the top of the bag, 1 piece 7 x 8in (18 x 20.5cm) for the pocket

1 fat quarter of contrast fabric: 2 pieces 18 x 6¼in (45.5 x 16cm) for the base of the bag, 1 piece 7 x 8in (18 x 20.5cm) for the pocket

105in (2.65m) of 1in (2.5cm)-wide webbing, cut in half

Tape measure or ruler

Sewing machine

Thread to match fabric

Sewing needle

Pins

Dress-making scissors

Pen or fabric marker

Iron

NOTE: You can make the bag from two fat quarters of the same fabric if you patch pieces together for the pocket. Remember that fat quarters are not always the same dimensions, so make paper templates and arrange them carefully on your fabric first to check you have enough material to make the bag.

1 Lay the two pocket pieces down right sides together. Pin together along one long edge and sew a $3/8$ in (1cm) seam by machine.

2 Turn your work right side out and press to make a sharp seam. Topstitch $1/8$in (3mm) from all edges to finish it off (see page 16).

3 Place one piece of top fabric in front of you, right side up. Position the pocket piece so that it is centred on the fabric and with its raw base edges aligned with the bottom. Tack in position.

4 Lay one piece of base fabric on top of the top fabric and pocket, right sides together. Position the edge of your base fabric so that it lies $3/4$in (2cm) above the raw bottom edge of your top fabric and pin or tack along this edge.

5 Sew a $3/8$in (1cm) seam along the edge of the base fabric by machine, passing over the bottom of the pocket. Fold the base fabric down over the seam and press the seam allowance towards the base. Turn the work over. Tuck $3/8$in (1cm) of the overhanging top fabric seam allowance over the base fabric seam allowance to encase its raw edges. Press with a hot iron and pin or tack in position.

6 Stitch a flat fell seam (two lines by machine) along this seam, $1/8$in (3mm) in from the original seam stitching and $1/8$in (3mm) from the edge you folded under. Turn over your work and press again.

7 Turn over your work again and fold over the top raw edge of the fabric by $3/8$in (1cm) and then $3/4$in (2cm) to make a neat hem. Pin or tack and stitch by machine.

8 Position one piece of webbing to form a handle on the right side of your work. Both bottom edges should butt up with the bottom edge of your base fabric, $6 1/4$in (15.75cm) apart. Pin the handle vertically to pass over the top edge of the fabric – the two sides of the handle should continue to lie $6 1/4$in (15.75cm) apart and cover the raw sides of the pocket. Stitch each side of the handle down by machine. Sew just in from the edge from the bottom to the top on one side, turning 90 degrees at the top of the bag and stitching along the width of the webbing several times for strength. Start stitching down the other side of the webbing, stopping at the level of the stitch line from step 7 – just short of $3/4$in (2cm) from the top edge. Turn 90 degrees and stitch along the width of the webbing several times for strength. Stitch down the remaining edge of webbing to the bottom of your work.

9 Stitch back and forth across the webbing again to align with the topstitching at the top of the pocket, for extra strength.

10 Repeat steps 4–9 with the remaining top and base pieces of fabric and handle. Place the two bag halves, wrong sides together. Align the edges and pin or tack, then sew a $3/8$in (1cm) seam all the way around.

11 Reverse stitch as you start and finish (see page 18). Trim the seam allowance to $3/16$in (5mm) and clip the bottom corners (see page 19).

12 Turn the bag inside out. Tease the seams all the way around to make them as sharp as you can and press with a hot iron. Pin or tack around both sides and the bottom edge. Sew a $3/8$in (1cm) seam all the way around, reverse stitching at the start and finish.

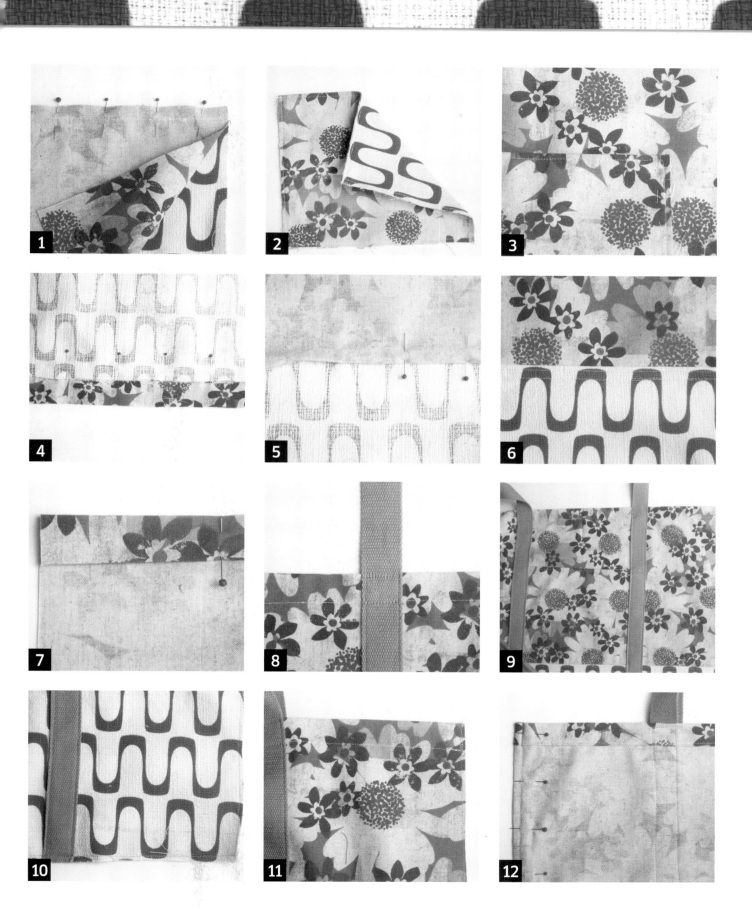

TEMPLATES

Templates that are shown at actual size (labelled as 100%) can be traced and cut out, or photocopied. For templates that have been reduced in size, enlarge them on an A3 photocopier to the percentage stated on the pattern pieces.

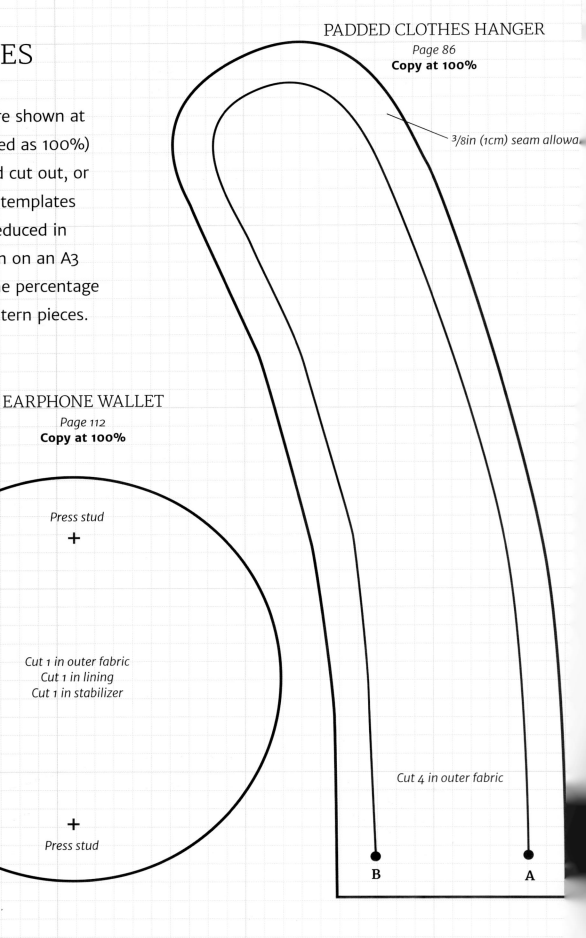

PADDED CLOTHES HANGER

Page 86
Copy at 100%

⅜in (1cm) seam allowa...

EARPHONE WALLET

Page 112
Copy at 100%

Press stud

+

Cut 1 in outer fabric
Cut 1 in lining
Cut 1 in stabilizer

+
Press stud

Cut 4 in outer fabric

B   **A**

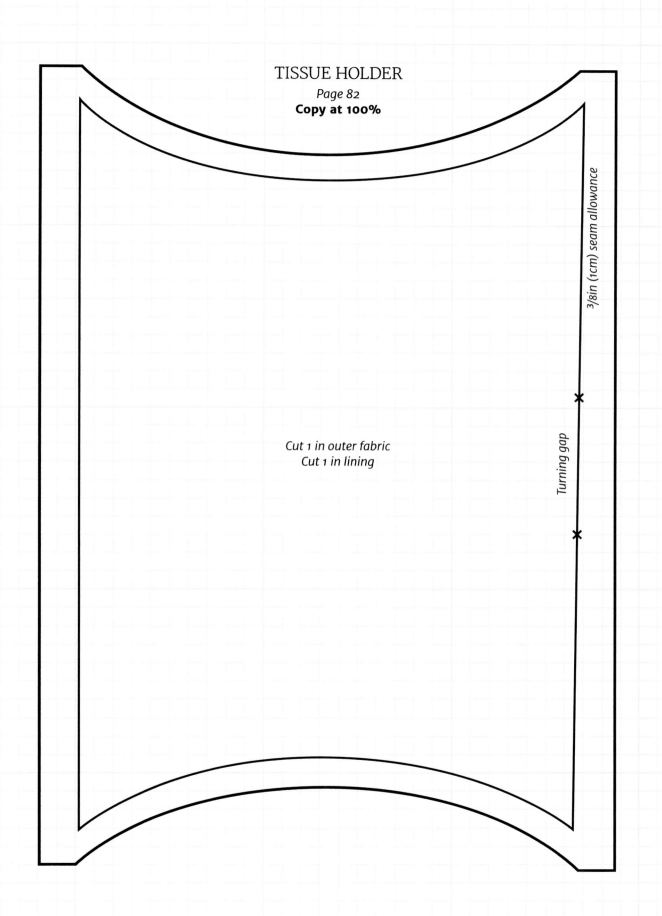

TISSUE HOLDER
Page 82
Copy at 100%

³/8in (1cm) seam allowance

✗

Turning gap

✗

Cut 1 in outer fabric
Cut 1 in lining

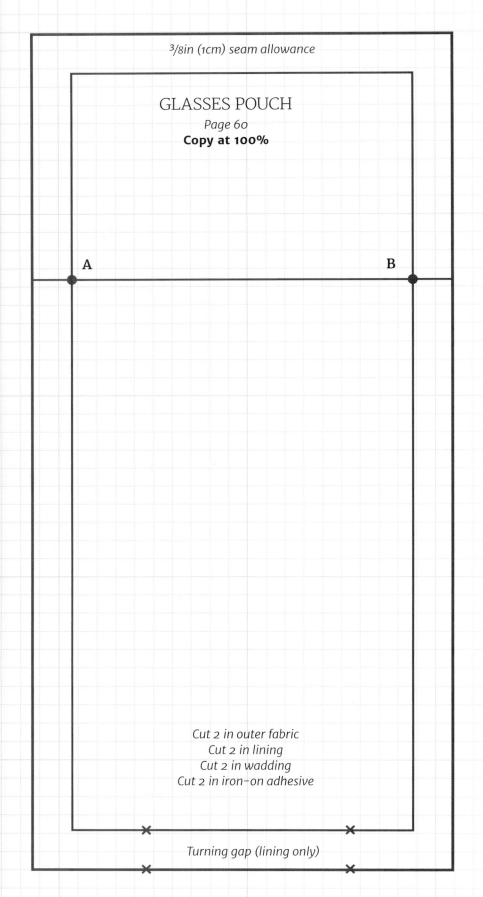

3/8in (1cm) seam allowance

GLASSES POUCH
Page 60
Copy at 100%

A

B

Cut 2 in outer fabric
Cut 2 in lining
Cut 2 in wadding
Cut 2 in iron-on adhesive

Turning gap (lining only)

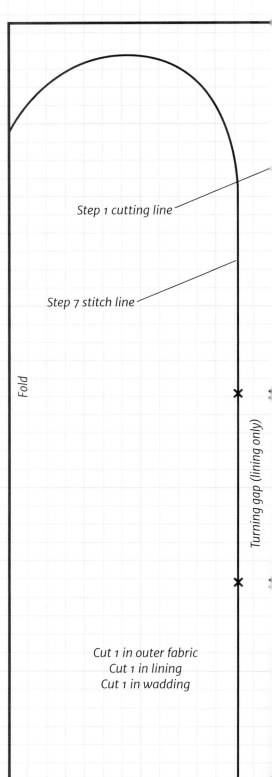

POT HANDLE SLEEVES
Page 34
Copy at 100%

Step 1 cutting line

Step 7 stitch line

Fold

Turning gap (lining only)

Cut 1 in outer fabric
Cut 1 in lining
Cut 1 in wadding

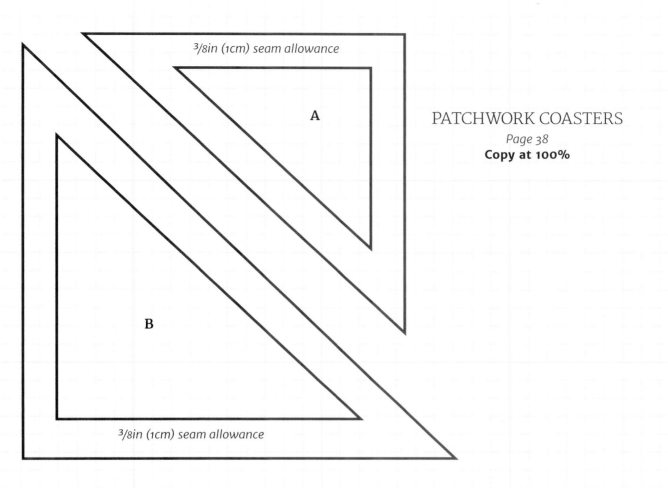

3/8in (1cm) seam allowance

A

B

3/8in (1cm) seam allowance

PATCHWORK COASTERS
Page 38
Copy at 100%

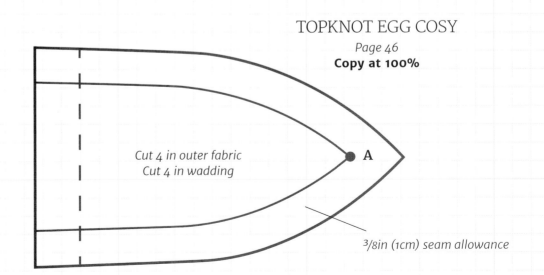

TOPKNOT EGG COSY
Page 46
Copy at 100%

Cut 4 in outer fabric
Cut 4 in wadding

A

3/8in (1cm) seam allowance

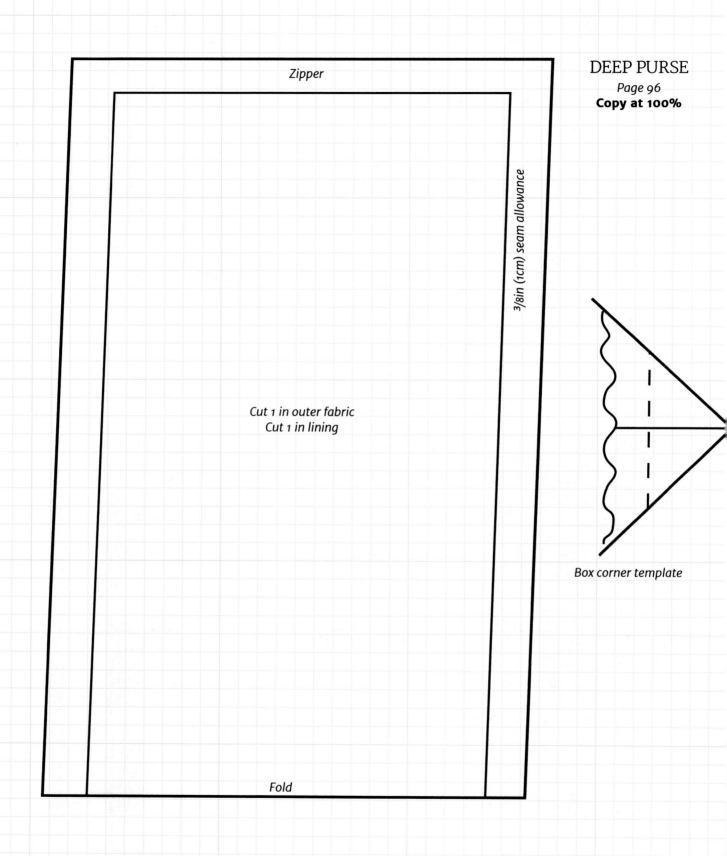

Zipper

DEEP PURSE
Page 96
Copy at 100%

³⁄₈in (1cm) seam allowance

Cut 1 in outer fabric
Cut 1 in lining

Box corner template

Fold

LAVENDER FLOWERS
Page 78
Copy at 100%

Cut 1

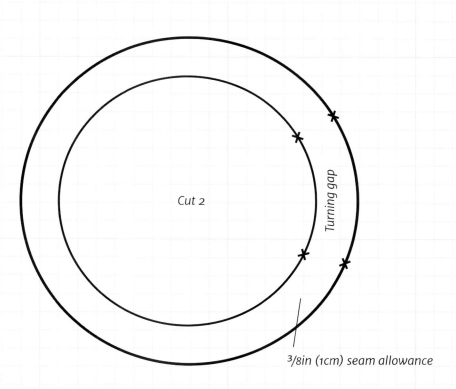

Cut 2

Turning gap

³/8in (1cm) seam allowance

PENCIL CASE
Page 56
Copy at 200%

Box corner template

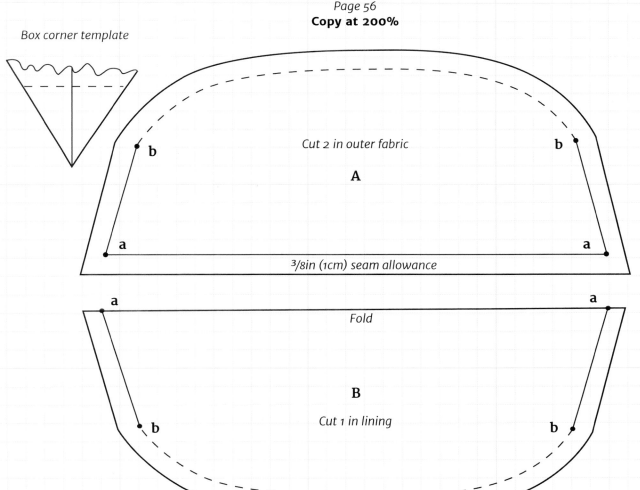

Cut 2 in outer fabric

A

b   b

a   a

³/8in (1cm) seam allowance

a   a

Fold

B

Cut 1 in lining

b   b

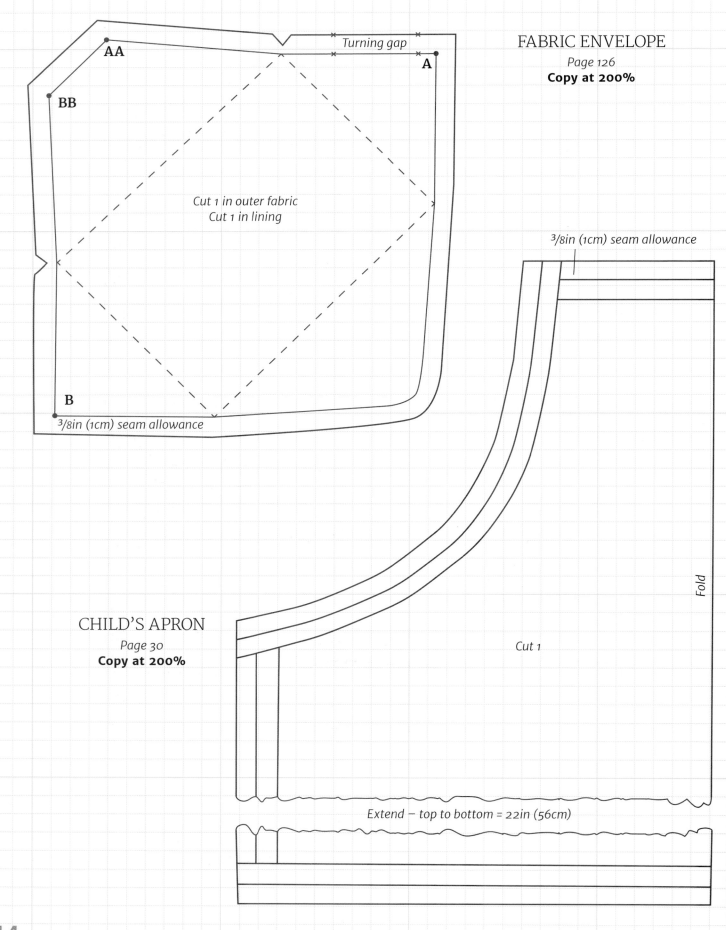

AA

BB

A

Turning gap

FABRIC ENVELOPE
Page 126
Copy at 200%

Cut 1 in outer fabric
Cut 1 in lining

⅜in (1cm) seam allowance

B

⅜in (1cm) seam allowance

CHILD'S APRON
Page 30
Copy at 200%

Fold

Cut 1

Extend – top to bottom = 22in (56cm)

HAIRBRUSH BAG
Page 90
Copy at 200%

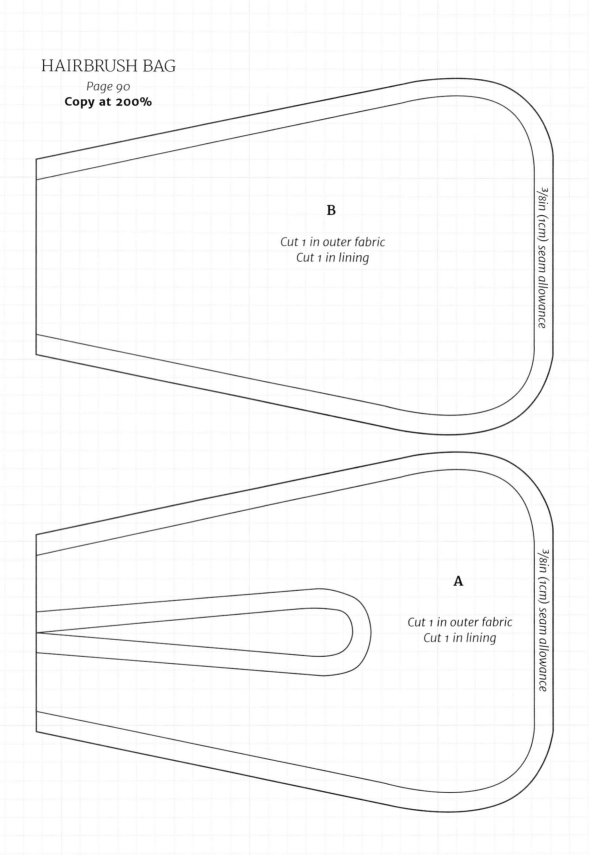

B

Cut 1 in outer fabric
Cut 1 in lining

3/8in (1cm) seam allowance

A

Cut 1 in outer fabric
Cut 1 in lining

3/8in (1cm) seam allowance

CARD WALLET
Page 130
Copy at 200%

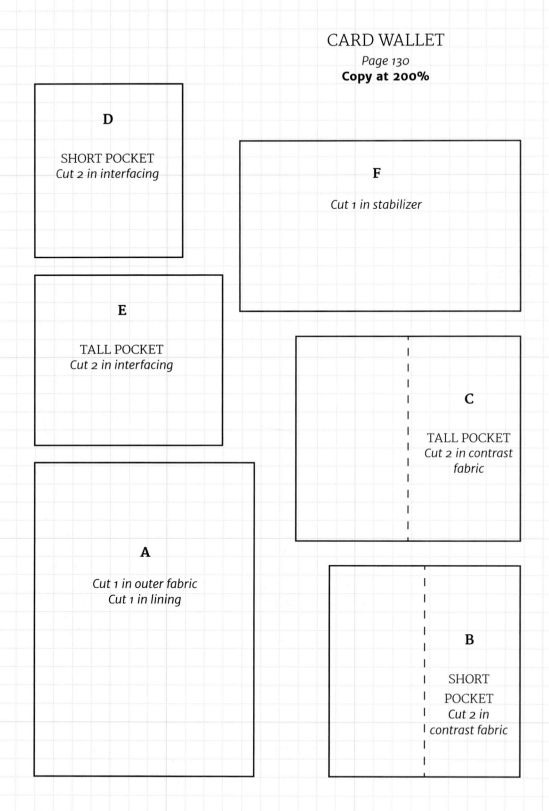

D

SHORT POCKET
Cut 2 in interfacing

F

Cut 1 in stabilizer

E

TALL POCKET
Cut 2 in interfacing

C

TALL POCKET
Cut 2 in contrast fabric

A

Cut 1 in outer fabric
Cut 1 in lining

B

SHORT POCKET
Cut 2 in contrast fabric

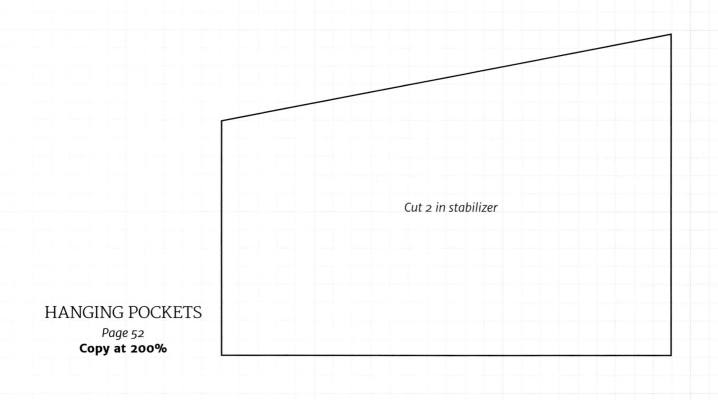

Cut 2 in stabilizer

HANGING POCKETS
Page 52
Copy at 200%

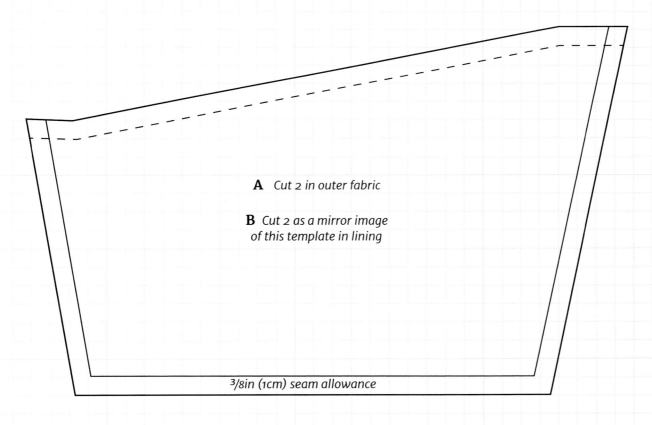

A Cut 2 in outer fabric

B Cut 2 as a mirror image
of this template in lining

³/8in (1cm) seam allowance

JEWELLERY POUCH

Page 118
Copy at 200%

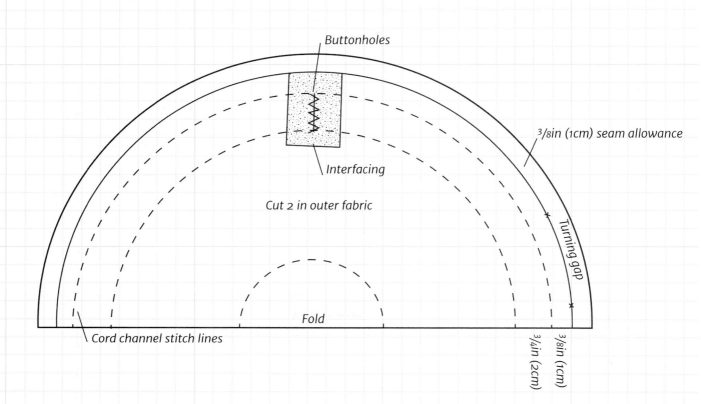

Buttonholes

³/8in (1cm) seam allowance

Interfacing

Cut 2 in outer fabric

Turning gap

Fold

Cord channel stitch lines

³/4in (2cm)

³/8in (1cm)

Cut 1 in stabilizer

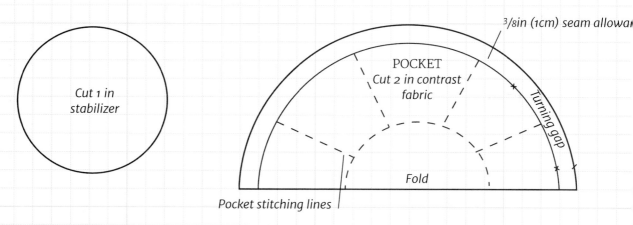

³/8in (1cm) seam allowan

POCKET
Cut 2 in contrast fabric

Turning gap

Fold

Pocket stitching lines

DRAWSTRING BAG

Page 122
Copy at 200%

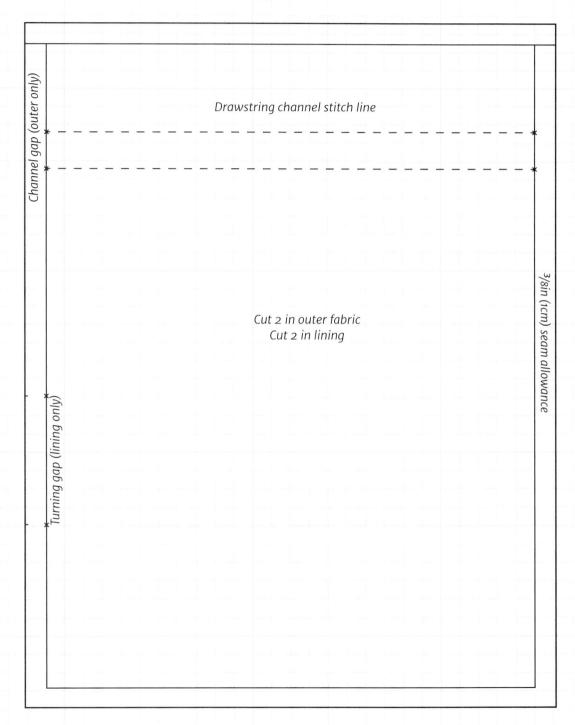

Channel gap (outer only)

Drawstring channel stitch line

3/8in (1cm) seam allowance

Cut 2 in outer fabric
Cut 2 in lining

Turning gap (lining only)

RESOURCES

Fabrics, wadding, interfacing, stabilizers
The Village Haberdashery
www.thevillagehaberdashery.co.uk

Flexi frame and 'D' rings
Bags Clasps
www.bag-clasps.co.uk

Key fob hardware, coat hangers, cushion pad
Amazon
www.amazon.co.uk

Towel
The White Company
www.thewhitecompany.co.uk

Haberdashery and scissors, zips, buttons, tapes, trim
The Brighton Sewing Centre
www.brightonsewingcentre.co.uk

Sewing machine
Janome
www.janome.co.uk

ACKNOWLEDGEMENTS

A big thank you to Emma Sekhon for the wonderful photography, as ever. To Gilda, Manisha, Jonathan, Cath, Sara and everyone at GMC for their input. Glenn for his persistent skills and care. My friends, my lovely family and especially Harrison and Martha.

INDEX

To order a book, or to request
a catalogue, contact:

GMC Publications Ltd
Castle Place, 166 High Street,
Lewes, East Sussex,
BN7 1XU
United Kingdom
Tel: +44 (0)1273 488005
www.gmcbooks.com